D0852975

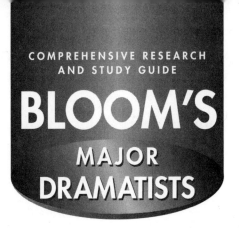

COMPREHENSIVE RESEARCH
AND STUDY GUIDE

BLOOM'S
MAJOR
DRAMATISTS

Shakespeare's
Comedies

EDITED AND WITH AN
INTRODUCTION BY HAROLD BLOOM

BLOOM'S MAJOR DRAMATISTS

Anton Chekhov
Henrik Ibsen
Arthur Miller
Eugene O'Neill
Shakespeare's Comedies
Shakespeare's Histories
Shakespeare's Romances
Shakespeare's Tragedies
George Bernard Shaw
Tennessee Williams

BLOOM'S MAJOR NOVELISTS

Jane Austen
The Brontës
Willa Cather
Charles Dickens
William Faulkner
F. Scott Fitzgerald
Nathaniel Hawthorne
Ernest Hemingway
Toni Morrison
John Steinbeck
Mark Twain
Alice Walker

BLOOM'S MAJOR SHORT STORY WRITERS

William Faulkner
F. Scott Fitzgerald
Ernest Hemingway
O. Henry
James Joyce
Herman Melville
Flannery O'Connor
Edgar Allan Poe
J. D. Salinger
John Steinbeck
Mark Twain
Eudora Welty

BLOOM'S MAJOR WORLD POETS

Geoffrey Chaucer
Emily Dickinson
John Donne
T. S. Eliot
Robert Frost
Langston Hughes
John Milton
Edgar Allan Poe
Shakespeare's Poems & Sonnets
Alfred, Lord Tennyson
Walt Whitman
William Wordsworth

BLOOM'S NOTES

The Adventures of Huckleberry Finn
Aeneid
The Age of Innocence
Animal Farm
The Autobiography of Malcolm X
The Awakening
Beloved
Beowulf
Billy Budd, Benito Cereno, & Bartleby the Scrivener
Brave New World
The Catcher in the Rye
Crime and Punishment
The Crucible

Death of a Salesman
A Farewell to Arms
Frankenstein
The Grapes of Wrath
Great Expectations
The Great Gatsby
Gulliver's Travels
Hamlet
Heart of Darkness & The Secret Sharer
Henry IV, Part One
I Know Why the Caged Bird Sings
Iliad
Inferno
Invisible Man
Jane Eyre
Julius Caesar

King Lear
Lord of the Flies
Macbeth
A Midsummer Night's Dream
Moby-Dick
Native Son
Nineteen Eighty-Four
Odyssey
Oedipus Plays
Of Mice and Men
The Old Man and the Sea
Othello
Paradise Lost
The Portrait of a Lady
A Portrait of the Artist as a Young Man

Pride and Prejudice
The Red Badge of Courage
Romeo and Juliet
The Scarlet Letter
Silas Marner
The Sound and the Fury
The Sun Also Rises
A Tale of Two Cities
Tess of the D'Urbervilles
Their Eyes Were Watching God
To Kill a Mockingbird
Uncle Tom's Cabin
Wuthering Heights

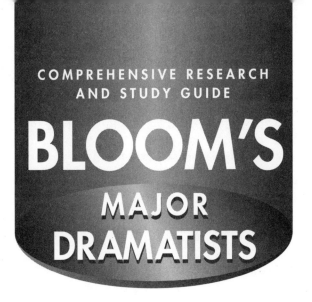

COMPREHENSIVE RESEARCH
AND STUDY GUIDE

BLOOM'S
MAJOR
DRAMATISTS

Shakespeare's Comedies

EDITED AND WITH AN INTRODUCTION
BY HAROLD BLOOM

First Printing
1 3 5 7 9 8 6 4 2

Library of Congress Cataloging-in-Publication Data
Shakespeare's comedies : comprehensive research and study guide /
    edited and with an introduction by Harold Bloom.
        p.   cm. — (Bloom's major dramatists)
    Includes bibliographical references and index.
    ISBN 0-7910-5238-9
    1. Shakespeare, William, 1564–1616—Comedies—Examinations Study
guides.   I. Bloom, Harold.   II. Series
PR2981.S498   1999
822.3′3—dc21   99–15681
                                                                CIP

822.33
Shak

Chelsea House Publishers
1974 Sproul Road, Suite 400
Broomall, PA 19008-0914

The Chelsea House World Wide Web address is
www.chelseahouse.com

Contributing Editor: Mirjana Kalezic

Contents

User's Guide

This volume is designed to present biographical, critical, and bibliographical information on the playwright's best-known or most important works. Following Harold Bloom's editor's note and introduction are a detailed biography of the author, discussing major life events and important literary accomplishments. A plot summary of each play follows, tracing significant themes, patterns, and motifs in the work.

A selection of critical extracts, derived from previously published material from leading critics, analyzes aspects of each play. The extracts consist of statements from the author, if available, early reviews of the work, and later evaluations up to the present. A bibliography of the author's writings (including a complete list of all works written, cowritten, edited, and translated), a list of additional books and articles on the author and his or her work, and an index of themes and ideas in the author's writings conclude the volume.

~

Harold Bloom is Sterling Professor of the Humanities at Yale University and Henry W. and Albert A. Berg Professor of English at the New York University Graduate School. He is the author of over 20 books and the editor of more than 30 anthologies of literary criticism.

Professor Bloom's works include *Shelley's Mythmaking* (1959), *The Visionary Company* (1961), *Blake's Apocalypse* (1963), *Yeats* (1970), *A Map of Misreading* (1975), *Kabbalah and Criticism* (1975), and *Agon: Toward a Theory of Revisionism* (1982). *The Anxiety of Influence* (1973) sets forth Professor Bloom's provocative theory of the literary relationships between the great writers and their predecessors. His most recent books include *The American Religion* (1992), *The Western Canon* (1994), *Omens of Millennium: The Gnosis of Angels, Dreams, and Resurrection* (1996), and *Shakespeare: The Invention of the Human* (1998), a finalist for the 1998 National Book Award.

Professor Bloom earned his Ph.D. from Yale University in 1955 and has served on the Yale faculty since then. He is a 1985 MacArthur Foundation Award recipient, served as the Charles Eliot Norton Professor of Poetry at Harvard University in 1987–88, and has received honorary degrees from the universities of Rome and Bologna. In 1999, Professor Bloom received the prestigious American Academy of Arts and Letters Gold Medal for Criticism.

Currently, Harold Bloom is the editor of numerous Chelsea House volumes of literary criticism, including the series BLOOM'S NOTES, BLOOM'S MAJOR SHORT STORY WRITERS, BLOOM'S MAJOR POETS, MAJOR LITERARY CHARACTERS, MODERN CRITICAL VIEWS, MODERN CRITICAL INTERPRETATIONS, and WOMEN WRITERS OF ENGLISH AND THEIR WORKS.

Editor's Note

The Critical Views reflect the main tradition of Shakespeare criticism from Dr. Samuel Johnson, Samuel Taylor Coleridge, and William Hazlitt to modern critics, including Harold C. Goddard, C. L. Barber, G. K. Chesterton, Anne Barton, Graham Bradshaw, G. Wilson Knight, Ruth Nevo, and the editor of this volume.

It might be objected that little here represents feminism, New Historicism, academic Marxism, and various fashionable Parisian modes of commentary. So be it. ❀

Introduction

HAROLD BLOOM

I

The greatness of Shakespeare's High Comedies—*A Midsummer Night's Dream, As You Like It, The Merchant of Venice,* and *Twelfth Night, or What You Will*—fully matches the magnificence of his four High Tragedies: *Hamlet, Othello, King Lear,* and *Macbeth.* Shakespeare's natural gift was for comedy; he is already fully himself in the early farces, *The Comedy of Errors* and *The Taming of the Shrew.* The shadow of Christopher Marlowe darkens *Titus Andronicus* and *Richard III,* but Marlowe had no interest and little talent for comedy. *The Tempest* is still essentially comedy, little as we tend to apprehend this.

II

A Midsummer Night's Dream is unique in Shakespeare, because it is the most visionary of his dramas, beyond even *The Tempest* as a transcendental enterprise. Ariel and the spirits are of another order of representation than are Puck, Titania, Oberon and Bottom's good friends: Cobweb, Mustardseed, Peaseblossom, and Moth, all elves of the greatest charm and amiability, worthy of the sublime Bottom himself. Of Bottom, no praise can be excessive. Ancestor of Joyce's Poldy Bloom, Bottom radiates good will and good sense; he is sound at the core, and is the skein upon which the play's elaborate designs is wound. One of Shakespeare's great originals, Bottom is not always well served by modern criticism, which tends to underestimate his innate dignity. Natural man, so much maligned by moralists, whether Christian or Marxist, achieves an apotheosis in Bottom.

And yet there is much more to Bottom than even that grand dignity. He alone, of the play's humans, is open to the realm of the fairies, and he alone enjoys the bottomless dream that in some sense is the ethos of Shakespeare's visionary play. Weavers are in touch with uncanny forces, and Bottom is the prince of weavers. He holds God's secrets, even if he is unaware of them. There is a link between Bottom's sweet good nature and the high, good spirits of Shakespeare's true genius Sir John Falstaff.

III

If Falstaff (and Hamlet) have a rival for audacious intelligence and slyly agile wit in all Shakespeare, then she must be the superb Rosalind, heroine of *As You Like It,* the most joyous of the comedies. The Forest of Arden may not be an earthly paradise, but in Shakespeare it is the best place to be, and Rosalind is the best person to be with in all of literature. William Hazlitt wonderfully said of Rosalind: "She talks herself out of breath, only to get deeper in love." I myself tend to emphasize her originality, in which she fully rivals Falstaff and Hamlet. In one crucial way, she transcends even them. As the audience, we can achieve perspectives upon Falstaff and Hamlet that are not available to them, but we enjoy no such privilege in regard to Rosalind. Dramatic irony can and does victimize Falstaff and Hamlet, but never Rosalind. She sees herself and her play all around, as it were; she arranges her own surprises. You cannot close the doors upon Rosalind's wit; it will out at the casement. Neither passive nor aggressive, Rosalind's wit is the subtlest I have encountered in literature.

IV

The Merchant of Venice, insofar as it is Portia's play, is high comedy, but history has made it Shylock's play also, which has rendered this great work highly problematic. Shylock's play can be done as farce, as tragicomedy, or as something for which we lack a name. One doesn't have to be Jewish to be horrified by forced conversion, on threat of death, to Christianity, but of course there is a particular shudder involved for Jewish playgoers and readers, like myself. What are we to do with *The Merchant of Venice?* Portia, though she squanders herself, is almost of Rosalind's splendor. Shylock's energy of being, the heroism of his malevolent will, and most of all his shattering eloquence: these combine to render him as memorable as he is frightening, a permanent slander against the Jewish people and its traditions of trusting to Yahwistic righteousness. I yield to no one in Bardolatry, but still must affirm that the role of Shylock has done grievous harm.

Yet *The Merchant of Venice* remains a masterwork of Shakespearean comedy, even if we do not laugh with it as Shakespeare's own audiences did. The ravishing Act V, set in Portia's Belmont, is a lyrical triumph, juxtaposing fulfilled Romantic love with ironic overtones of love's betrayal. Shylock's absence in the final act is both a tribute to the sophisticated power of Portia's world, and a critique of its limitations.

V

Of Shakespeare's early farces, *The Taming of the Shrew* maintains a perpetual popularity. The loving struggle for supremacy between Kate and Petruchio is an epitome of a crucial element in nearly every marriage, and the war between men and women is of universal relevance. It is too easy to get this play quite wrong; there are feminist visions of the "brutal" Petruchio pursuing Kate with a whip! In mere fact, she slaps him, and he confines his assaults to language. What Shakespeare actually gives us is the subtle self-education of Kate, who achieves dominion over the swaggering Petruchio through a parody of submission. What is profoundly moving is the representation of two ferocious beings who fall in love at first sight (though Kate conceals it) and who eventually make a strong alliance against the rest of the world. Beneath the surface of this knockabout farce, Shakespeare pursues one of his most illuminating contentions: the natural superiority of women over men.

VI

Twelfth Night is Shakespeare's farewell to high comedy, and may be his greatest achievement in that mode. Whose play is it; does it center upon Viola, Olivia, Malvolio, or Feste? That is rather like asking whether *King Lear* centers upon Edmund, the Fool, Edgar, or Lear himself. A beautifully complex comedy, *Twelfth Night* refuses the perspective that would make it poor, victimized Malvolio's tragicomedy. Like Shylock, Malvolio is one of Shakespeare's displaced spirits; he is not at home in the comic world of the play. And yet the play *needs* Malvolio; his undeserved downfall is essential to Shakespeare's vision. There is no poetic justice (or Christian consolation) in Shakespeare: the whirligig of time accomplishes its revenges. A delight and a madness, *Twelfth Night*'s only sane character is the remarkable Feste, the most admirable of Shakespeare's clowns. Viola is benign and lovable, yet she is as much a zany as Orsino, whom she will marry, or Olivia, who rarely gets anything straight. *Twelfth Night*, a sublime Feast of Fools, is as crowning an achievement as are *King Lear* and *The Tempest*, all summits of their mode. ❀

Biography of
William Shakespeare

William Shakespeare was born in Stratford-on-Avon in April 1564 into a family of some prominence. His father, John Shakespeare, was a glover and merchant of leather goods, who earned enough to marry the daughter of his father's landlord, Mary Arden, in 1557. John Shakespeare was a prominent citizen in Stratford, and at one point, he served as an alderman and bailiff.

Shakespeare presumably attended the Stratford grammar school, where he would have received an education in Latin, but he did not go on to either Oxford or Cambridge universities. Little is recorded about Shakespeare's early life; indeed, the first record of his life after his christening is of his marriage to Anne Hathaway in 1582 in the church at Temple Grafton, near Stratford. He would have been required to obtain a special license from the bishop as security that there was no impediment to the marriage. Peter Alexander states in his book *Shakespeare's Life and Art* that marriage at this time in England required neither a church nor a priest or, for that matter, even a document—only a declaration of the contracting parties in the presence of witnesses. Thus, it was customary, though not mandatory, to follow the marriage with a church ceremony.

Little is known about William and Anne Shakespeare's marriage. Their first child, Susanna, was born in May 1583, and twins, Hamnet and Judith Shakespeare, in 1585. Later on, Susanna married Dr. John Hall, but the younger daughter, Judith, remained unmarried. When Hamnet died in Stratford in 1596, the boy was only eleven years old.

We have no record of Shakespeare's activities for the seven years after the birth of his twins, but by 1592 he was in London working as an actor. He was also apparently well-known as a playwright, for reference is made of him by his contemporary, Robert Greene, in *A Groatsworth of Wit,* as "an upstart crow."

Several companies of actors were in London at this time. Shakespeare may have had connection with one or more of them before 1592, but we have no record that tells us definitely. However, we do know of his long association with the most famous and successful troupe, the Lord Chamberlain's Men. (When James I came to the throne in 1603, after Elizabeth's death, the troupe's name changed to the King's Men.) In 1599 the Lord Chamberlain's Men provided the financial backing for the construction of their own theatre, the Globe.

The Globe was begun by a carpenter named James Burbage and finished by his two sons, Cuthbert and Robert. To escape the jurisdiction of the Corporation of London, which was composed of conservative Puritans who opposed the theatre's "licentiousness," James Burbage built the Globe just outside London, in the Liberty of Holywell, beside Finsbury Fields. This also meant that the Globe was safer from the threats that lurked in London's crowded streets, like plague and other diseases, as well as rioting mobs. When James Burbage died in 1598, his sons completed the Globe's construction. Shakespeare played a vital role, financially and otherwise, in the construction of the theater, which was finally occupied some time before May 16, 1599.

Shakespeare not only acted with the Globe's company of actors; he was also a shareholder and eventually became the troupe's most important playwright. The company included London's most famous actors, who inspired the creation of Shakespeare's well-known characters such as Hamlet and Lear, as well as his clowns and fools.

In his early years, however, Shakespeare did not confine himself to the theatre. He also composed some mythological-erotic poetry, such as *Venus and Adonis* and *The Rape of Lucrece,* both of which were dedicated to the earl of Southampton. Shakespeare was successful enough that in 1597 he was able to purchase his own home in Stratford, which he called New Place. He could even call himself a gentleman, for his father had been granted a coat of arms.

By 1598 Shakespeare had written some of his most famous works, *Romeo and Juliet, The Comedy of Errors, A Midsummer Night's Dream, The Merchant of Venice, Two Gentleman of Verona, and Love's Labor Lost,* as well as his historical plays *Richard II, Richard III, Henry IV,* and *King John.* Somewhere around the turn of the century, Shakespeare wrote his romantic comedies, *As You Like It, Twelfth Night,* and *Much Ado About Nothing,* as well as *Henry V,* the last of his history plays in the Prince Hal series. During the next ten years he wrote his great tragedies, *Hamlet, Macbeth, Othello, King Lear,* and *Antony and Cleopatra.*

At this time, the theatre was burgeoning in London; the public took an avid interest in drama, the audiences were large, the plays demonstrated an enormous range of variety, and playwrights competed for approval. By 1613, however, the rising tide of Puritanism had changed the theatre. With the desertion of the theatres by the middle classes, the acting companies were compelled to depend more on the aristocracy, which also meant that they now had to cater to a more sophisticated audience.

Perhaps this change in London's artistic atmosphere contributed to Shakespeare's reasons for leaving London after 1612. His retirement from the theatre is sometimes thought to be evidence that his artistic skills were waning. During this time, however, he wrote *The Tempest* and *Henry VIII*. He also wrote the "tragicomedies," *Pericles, Cymbeline,* and *The Winter's Tale.* These were thought to be inspired by Shakespeare's personal problems, and have sometimes been considered proof of his greatly diminished abilities.

However, so far as biographical facts indicate, the circumstances of his life at this time do not imply any personal problems. He was in good health, financially secure, and enjoyed an excellent reputation. Indeed, although he was settled in Stratford at this time, he made frequent visits to London, enjoying and participating in events at the royal court, directing rehearsals, and attending to other business matters.

In addition to his brilliant and enormous contributions to the theatre, Shakespeare remained a poetic genius throughout the years, publishing a well-renowned and critically-acclaimed sonnet cycle in 1609. Shakespeare's contribution to this popular poetic genre are all the more amazing in his break with contemporary notions of subject matter. Shakespeare idealized the beauty of man as an object of praise and devotion (rather than the Petrarchan tradition of the idealized, unattainable woman). In the same spirit of breaking with tradition, Shakespeare also treated themes which hitherto had been considered off limits—the dark, sexual side of a woman as opposed to the Petrarchan ideal of a chaste and remote love object. He also expanded the sonnet's emotional range, including such emotions as delight, pride, shame, disgust, sadness, and fear.

When Shakespeare died in 1616, no collected edition of his works had ever been published, although some of his plays had been printed in separate unauthorized editions. (Some of these were taken from his manuscripts, some from the actors' prompt books, and others were reconstructed from memory by actors or spectators.) In 1623, two members of the King's Men, John Hemings and Henry Condell, published a collection of all the plays they considered to be authentic, the First Folio.

Included in the First Folio is a poem by Shakespeare's contemporary Ben Jonson, an outstanding playwright and critic in his own right. Jonson paid tribute to Shakespeare's genius, proclaiming his superiority to what previously had been held as the models for literary excellence—the Greek and Latin writers. "Triumph, my Britain, thou hast one to show / To whom all scenes of Europe homage owe. / He was not of an age, but for all time!"

Jonson was the first to state what has been said so many times since. Having captured what is permanent and universal to all human beings at all times, Shakespeare's genius continues to inspire us—and the critical debate about his works never ceases.

Plot Summary of
The Taming of the Shrew

The Taming of the Shrew must have been written in 1593–1594, after *Two Gentlemen of Verona* (1592–1593) and before *A Midsummer Night's Dream* (1595–1596). Even in this early comedy, Shakespeare proves to be a master of plot construction. He integrates two distinct plot lines, each derived from a different source, into a work of structural and thematic unity. The source for the main plot—Petruchio's taming of Kate—is most probably an anonymous play entitled *The Taming of a Shrew*. There are undeniable elements of farce in the Kate/Petruchio story. Most scholars agree that the Bianca plot line is derived from George Gascoigne's *Supposes* (acted 1566, published 1573), actually a translation of an Italian play, Ariosto's *I Suppositi*. The recurring theme in all of Shakespeare's early comedies, and the central theme of this play, is the deceptiveness of appearances, the difference between semblance and reality, and the exchange of identities. *The Taming of the Shrew* is the only play that has an "induction," an initial section that introduces the main action to come later.

In the induction Shakespeare gives us a framework for the play. A noble lord, returning from the hunt, comes across Christopher Sly, a beggar who has just been thrown out of an alehouse. He is dead-drunk and asleep. The lord decides to play a trick on him and carries him to his house. Sly wakens surrounded by wealth and comfort. He is told that he is a great lord who, after a long time, has come back to his senses. Sly yields to this illusion: not only does he accept the external circumstances, but he also adopts the personality of a lord. This is another of Shakespeare's touches on the exchange of identities. When the troupe of traveling actors comes, they present the play (which is actually the play within the play) *The Taming of the Shrew*. Sly will interrupt the play only once, and after that Shakespeare does not bring his character back. In such a brief period of time Christopher Sly is endowed with so much individuality that we miss him throughout the rest of the play.

In **Act I,** scene one a young man, Lucentio, arrives with his servant, Tranio, to Padua to study. Upon their arrival they witness a scene between Baptista and his two daughters, Kate and Bianca, accompanied by Gremio and Hortensio, Bianca's suitors. Baptista proclaims that he will not give permission for his younger daughter, Bianca, to get married, until Kate marries first. Bianca is presented as sweet tempered while Kate, although beautiful, is such a shrew that no suitor would come close to her. Baptista asks Gremio and Hortensio to find a husband for Kate as well as tutors for both of his daughters. Lucentio falls immediately in love with Bianca.

In scene two Petruchio, a nobleman from Verona, comes to Padua. His friend Hortensio confesses his love for Bianca and suggests that Petruchio woo Kate. Petruchio agrees without much thought. Hortensio plans to disguise himself as a music teacher with the name Litio. At this point, the plot gets confusing: Lucentio is disguised as Cambio, a teacher of languages, so that he can woo Bianca, while his servant, Tranio, is dressed as Lucentio.

Act II, scene one finds Bianca with her hands tied and Kate beating her, demanding to know which of the suitors she likes best. Baptista interferes. Petruchio visits Baptista and presents Hortensio (as Litio). Gremio introduces Lucentio (as Cambio), while Tranio (as Lucentio) declares his wish to marry Bianca. Petruchio asks for Kate's hand, but Baptista asks him to court her first. His speedy courtship consists of an exchange of shocking words with Kate, in which she calls him a "lunatic" and a "swearing Jack." Petruchio persuades Baptista that Kate just pretends not to like him in public, and Kate's wedding date is set. Gremio and Tranio (disguised as Lucentio) now compete for Bianca's hand. Gremio is outvied, however, because Tranio can claim more ducats, more houses, and more fruitful land. Baptista therefore awards Bianca to Tranio (Lucentio) under the condition that Vincentio, Lucentio's father, guarantees the dowry to Bianca, in case Lucentio (i.e., Tranio) dies before she does. Bianca's wedding is scheduled to take place the Sunday after Kate's. Tranio, as Lucentio, sets out to find a father, a "supposed Vincentio."

Act III, scene one takes place one day before Kate's wedding. Lucentio (as Cambio) and Hortensio (as Litio) continue to woo Bianca. Hortensio finds Cambio more common than himself and, left alone on the stage, declares that he will quit wooing Bianca and turn to someone else if Bianca allows anyone else to capture her heart.

The plot introduces many swerves on Kate's wedding day (scene two). Petruchio, for one, is late for his own wedding. When he shows, in tattered clothes with a new hat, he acts as if he were a real madman. He refuses to stay for supper following the wedding, and takes Kate with him to his country house.

Act IV, scene one brings us to Petruchio's country house, when Grumio (not Gremio), Petruchio's servant, tells Curtis about his master and his new wife's exciting trip home. Besides attacking the servants, hurling dinner plates, scolding and complaining, Petruchio denies Kate food and sleep. As the scene closes, he confides to the audience that "this is to way to kill a wife with kindness," and in a speech peppered with technical terms, he compares the taming of a wife with the training of a falcon.

Scene two finds Hortensio (as Litio) and Tranio (as Lucentio) in Padua, spying on Bianca and Lucentio (as Cambio), who are obviously in love with one another. Hortensio, in revolt of women's fickleness, removes his disguise and declares that he will marry a wealthy widow. In the meantime, Biondello, Tranio's servant, finds a merchant who can play the part of Lucentio's father for a meeting with Baptista.

In scene three the "taming" of Kate proceeds. Petruchio finally serves food to Kate, and then demands her thankfulness. He refuses to admit the haberdasher and the tailor who bring the cap and gown that Kate wants to wear to her sister's wedding. He also demands that she agree with everything he says, no matter how wrong he may be. If she doesn't, he indicates, she will never reach her father's house for the wedding.

Scene four shows us the merchant dressed like Vincentio. He visits Baptista to argue Tremio's (still dressed as Lucentio) cause. After the merchant guarantees Bianca's dowry, Baptista promises his daughter to Tranio (as Lucentio), and he intends to visit Tranio (as Lucentio) and his supposed father, Vincentio, in their lodging, in order to finish their business privately.

On their way to Padua (scene five), Kate and Petruchio meet the real Vincentio, who is traveling there to visit his son, Lucentio.

In **Act V,** the knots of the plot are untied. Bianca and the real Lucentio (who plays the teacher, Cambio) secretly marry in scene one. Petruchio, Kate, and the real father (Vincentio) arrive at Lucentio's lodging. When Vincentio knocks loudly on the door, the merchant looks out the window. Vincentio asks for his son Lucentio, but the merchant answers that he is in but not to be disturbed. Tranio, still disguised as Lucentio, appears after Vincentio proceeds to beat his servant. The real Vincentio is then proclaimed a lunatic and is nearly carried to jail. But the real Lucentio appears with Bianca at this point and explains the confusion. He asks for his father's forgiveness.

In the final banquet scene (**Act V,** scene two) all threads of the plot material are woven back together. The three newly wed men (Petruchio, Lucentio, and Hortensio, who had married a widow) wager on whose wife is the most obedient. Bianca had already begun to reveal a streak of willfulness and arrogance; as it turns out, Lucentio has married the shrewish sister. When they summon their wives, only Kate (now well tamed) appears instantly. Petruchio triumphs, and Kate brings Bianca and the widow along with her. As the play comes to a close, Kate delivers a long speech (which has been much discussed) in which she praises a woman's submission to her husband. ❀

List of Characters in
The Taming of the Shrew

Christopher Sly is a beggar who deliberately accepts having a trick played on him. He agrees to watch the play *The Taming of the Shrew*. His only comment comes after the end of the first scene, "Would 'twere done!" We never hear from him again.

Baptista Minola is a wealthy gentleman of Padua. He is the father of Kate, the "shrew," and Bianca, a gentle-tempered woman. He favors Bianca, his young daughter, but makes her marriage depend on that of Kate's.

Kate, "the shrew," is the elder daughter of Baptista. She marries Petruchio, who tames her by using crude methods. Unlike later female characters in Shakespeare's works, Kate has been sketched in bold strokes. In her concluding speech Kate argues for the total submission of wives to their husbands.

Bianca is the younger and favorite daughter of Baptista. Her plot is of secondary importance in the play. She is presented as sweet tempered but actually is not. She is wooed by Hortensio and Gremio, but Lucentio wins her heart.

Petruchio is a gentleman from Verona who is determined to marry and tame Kate, "the shrew." Even before he sees Kate, he asserts his method. He establishes his dominance throughout the play and eventually "kills her with her own humor."

Gremio is a rich but old suitor of Bianca, who is outvied by Tranio for Bianca's hand. He describes splendidly Petruchio's and Kate's relationship in Act III, scene two.

Hortensio is Bianca's suitor and a friend of Petruchio. He persuades Petruchio to marry Kate so that he can wed Bianca. He disguises himself as the teacher Litio in order to be close to Bianca. But revolted by her fickleness and a sensible man, he decides he is better off marrying a rich widow.

Lucentio is a young student from Pisa who comes to Padua to study. He falls in love with Bianca and, disguised as the teacher Cambio, skillfully and successfully woos her. They secretly marry.

- **Vincentio** is an old gentleman of Pisa, the father of Lucentio, who comes to Padua to visit his son. He is proclaimed a madman and almost carried off to prison after the confrontation with the merchant who is pretending to be Vincentio.

- **Tranio** is another servant of Lucentio. He disguises himself as Lucentio and becomes a competitor for Bianca's hand. This forms the subplot of the play.

- **Biondello** is a servant to Lucentio and plays the role of aide-de-camp who finds the merchant to play Lucentio's (i.e., Tranio's) supposed father.

A **merchant** plays the role of Lucentio's father, Vincentio, to help Tranio guarantee Bianca the dower, at the request of her father.

Grumio is Petruchio's servant who dishes it out to other servants or takes it from Petruchio. ❁

Critical Views on
The Taming of the Shrew

[August Wilhelm Schlegel (1767–1845) was a German
scholar and critic, and one of the most influential advocates
of the German Romantic movement. He was also an Orientalist and a poet. His greatest achievement is his translation
of Shakespeare. In his famous book *Lectures on Dramatic Art
and Literature (1809–1811),* excerpted here, Schlegel praises
the prelude more than the play itself.]

The Taming of the Shrew has the air of an Italian comedy; and indeed
the love intrigue, which constitutes the main part of it, is derived me-
diately or immediately from a piece of Ariosto. The characters and
passions are lightly sketched; the intrigue is introduced without much
preparation, and in its rapid progress impeded by no sort of difficul-
ties; while, in the manner in which Petruchio, though previously cau-
tioned as to Katherine, still encounters the risks in marrying her, and
contrives to tame her—in all this the character and peculiar humour
of the English are distinctly visible. The colours are laid on somewhat
coarsely, but the ground is good. That the obstinacy of a young and
untamed girl, possessed of none of the attractions of her sex, and neither supported by bodily nor mental strength, must soon yield to the
still rougher and more capricious but assumed self-will of a man: such
a lesson can only be taught on the stage with all the perspicuity of a
proverb.

The prelude is still more remarkable than the play itself: a drunken
tinker, removed in his sleep to a palace, where he is deceived into the
belief of being a nobleman. The invention, however, is not Shakespeare's. Holberg has handled the same subject in a masterly manner, and with inimitable truth; but he has spun it out to five acts, for
which such material is hardly sufficient. He probably did not borrow
from the English dramatist, but like him took the hint from a popular story. There are several comic motives of this description, which
go back to a very remote age, without ever becoming antiquated.

Here, as well as everywhere else, Shakespeare has proved himself a great poet: the whole is merely a slight sketch, but in elegance and delicate propriety it will hardly ever be excelled. Neither has he overlooked the irony which the subject naturally suggested: the great lord, who is driven by idleness and ennui to deceive a poor drunkard, can make no better use of his situation than the latter, who every moment relapses into his vulgar habits. The last half of this prelude, that in which the tinker, in his new state, again drinks himself out of his senses, and is transformed in his sleep into his former condition, is from some accident or other, lost. It ought to have followed at the end of the larger piece. The occasional remarks of the tinker, during the course of the representation of the comedy, might have been improvisatory; but it is hardly credible that Shakespeare should have trusted to the momentary suggestions of the players, whom he did not hold in high estimation, the conclusion, however short, of a work which he had so carefully commenced. Moreover, the only circumstance which connects the play with the prelude, is, that it belongs to the new life of the supposed nobleman to have plays acted in his castle by strolling actors. This invention of introducing spectators on the stage, who contribute to the entertainment, has been very wittily used by later English poets.

—August Wilhelm Schlegel, *Lectures on Dramatic Art and Literature*, trans. John Black (London: George Bell & Sons, 1886): pp. 381–382.

G. WILSON KNIGHT ON THE SHAKESPEAREAN TEMPEST

[G. Wilson Knight (1897–1985), a leading British Shakespeare scholar, taught drama and English literature at the University of Leeds. He was the author of many volumes of criticism, including *The Starlit Dome* (1941), *The Crown of Life* (1947), and *Shakespeare and Religion* (1967). In this extract from *The Shakespearean Tempest* (1932), Knight asserts that the Shakespearean tempest is the conflict of the beast and the angel in man; he explores it in the Petruchio-Katharina relationship.]

I pass to the story of Petruchio and Katharina. Petruchio's story may be told in terms of tempests. He is a strong man who boasts:

> Have I not in my time heard lions roar?
> Have I not heard the sea puff'd up with winds
> Rage like an angry boar chafed with sweat?
> Have I not heard great ordnance in the field,
> And heaven's artillery thunder in the skies?
>
> (I.ii.201)

Notice the beasts: 'lions', the 'angry boar', and the usual word 'chafed'. Elsewhere a man 'rages' like 'a chafed bull' and threatens 'death' (*3 Henry VI*, II.V. 126–7). Notice especially here the close tempest-boar association. We may remember how in *Venus and Adonis* love's tragedy is brought about by 'an angry-chafing boar' (*Venus and Adonis*, 662). Now Petruchio's fight is pre-eminently a fight with a tempest. Katharina is a 'wild-cat' –another tempest beast: 'Will you woo this wild-cat?' (I.ii.197) asks Gremio. Again,

> For I am he am born to tame you, Kate,
> And bring you from a wild Kate to a Kate
> Conformable as other household Kates.
>
> (II.i.270)

Here again, as in the Induction, we are pointed to a contrast between the bestial and the spiritual in humanity. Katharina is also like a tempest:

> . . . Mark'd you not how her sister
> Began to scold and raise up such a storm
> That mortal ears might hardly endure the din?
>
> (I.i.176)

But Petruchio will woo her though she be as 'rough'

> As are the swelling Adriatic seas.
>
> (I.ii.73)

Again, when Hortensio says he 'would not wed her for a mine of gold', Petruchio replies:

> Hortensio, peace! thou know'st not gold's effect:
> Tell me her father's name and 'tis enough;
> For I will board her, though she chide as loud
> As thunder when the clouds in autumn crack.
>
> (I.ii.93)

'Board' is a usual Shakespearean metaphor for any human encounter. He will meet her 'fire' like a blast of wind whose 'extreme gusts' will blow it out, for he is as 'peremptory as she proud-minded' (II.i.132). 'Peremptory' we have met before. So he goes to her armed

> as mountains are for winds,
> That shake not though they blow perpetually.
> (II.i.141)

Mountains, with their 'pines', are elsewhere found in tempest passages, resisting 'winds'. Katharina's temper is indeed tempestuous. It is like 'frosts' or 'whirlwinds' spoiling beauty's flower, stirring up her crystal beauty like a muddy stream. These 'frosts' and 'whirlwinds' suggest the close relation of all wintry effects to tempests. Her temper

> . . . blots thy beauty as frosts do bite the meads,
> Confounds thy frame as whirlwinds shake fair buds,
> And in no sense is meet or amiable.
> A woman moved is like a fountain troubled,
> Muddy, ill-seeming, thick, bereft of beauty;
> And while it is so, none so dry or thirsty,
> Will deign to sip or touch one drop of it.
> (V.ii.139)

So speaks Katharina at the end. But first she has to be conquered.

Throughout Petruchio behaves with shipman's manners. At the moment of his first victory at the church, having married her, he aptly celebrates his central success like a sailor after a tempest:

> 'A health!' quoth he, as if
> He had been aboard, carousing to his mates
> After a storm.
> (III.ii.172)

Such an image at so especially a crucial point—it is the same in *Timon*—seems to suggest that the poet, even when actual tempests are not present, yet is all the time, as it were, seeing his story as a sea-adventure. And this tempest-victory is naturally accompanied by music:

> Such a mad marriage never was before:
> Hark, hark! I hear the minstrels play. *Music*
> (III.ii.184)

So, at the close, Katharina recognizes the strong masculine power that, being made to fight the tempests of existence, gives man the right and prerogative of tempestuous behaviour. A husband is

> one that cares for thee,
> And for thy maintenance commits his body

To painful labour both by sea and land,
To watch the night in storms, the day in cold,
Whilst thou liest warm at home, secure and safe.

(V.ii.147)

Another cold-storm association: all bleak effects blend with tempests.

—G. Wilson Knight, *The Shakespearean Tempest* (London: Methuen, 1932): pp. 107–109.

MAYNARD MACK ON ENGAGEMENT AND DETACHMENT

[Maynard Mack was Sterling Professor of English at Yale University. He is the author of studies on Alexander Pope and Shakespeare. This extract, taken from his essay "Engagement and Detachment in Shakespeare's Plays," analyzes the characters of Sly and Petruchio.]

Finally, toward the beginning of Shakespeare's career, we have Sly in *The Taming of the Shrew*. Even in the anonymous play *A Shrew*, but much more in Shakespeare's version, we confront in Sly's experience after being thrown out of the alehouse what appears to be an abstract and brief chronicle of how stage illusion takes effect. Sly, having fallen briefly into one of those mysterious sleeps that Shakespeare elsewhere attributes to those who are undergoing the power of a dramatist, wakes to find the identity of a rich lord thrust upon him, rejects it at first, knowing perfectly well who he is ("Christopher Sly, old Sly's son, of Burton-heath. . . . Ask Marian Hacket, the fat ale-wife of Wincot, if she know me not"–Induction, 2.17–22), then is engulfed by it, accepts the dream as reality, accepts also a dressed-up players' boy to share the new reality with him as his supposed lady, and at last sits down with her beside him to watch the strolling players put on *The Taming of the Shrew*. Since Sly's newly assumed identity has no result whatever except to bring him face to face with a play, it is tempting to imagine him a witty paradigm of all of us as theatergoers, when we awake out of our ordinary reality of the alehouse, or whatever other reality ordinarily encompasses us, to the superimposed reality of the playhouse, and find that there (at any rate, so long as a comedy is playing) wishes are horses and beggars do ride. Sly, to be sure, soon disengages himself from the strollers' play and falls asleep; but in Shakespeare's version—the situation differs somewhat in *A Shrew*—his engagement to his identity as a lord, though presumably broken when the play ends, stretches into infinity for anything we are ever told.

This way of considering Sly is the more tempting in that the play as a whole manipulates the theme of displaced identity in a way that can hardly be ignored. For what the Lord and his Servants do in thrusting a temporary identity on Sly is echoed in what Petruchio does for Kate at a deeper level of psychic change. His gambits in taming her are equally displacements of identity: first, in thrusting on himself the rude self-will which actually belongs to her, so that she beholds what she now is in his mirror, and he (to quote his man Peter) "kills her in her own humor" (4.1.174); and second, in thrusting on her the semblance of a modest, well-conducted young woman.

—Maynard Mack, "Engagement and Detachment in Shakespeare's Plays," in *Essays on Shakespeare and Elizabethan Drama in Honor of Hardin Craig,* ed. Richard Hosley (Columbia, MO: University of Missouri Press, 1962): pp. 279–80.

Ruth Nevo on Comic Transformation

[Ruth Nevo, formerly a professor of English at the University of Jerusalem, is the author of *Comic Transformation in Shakespeare* (1980) and *Shakespeare's Other Language* (1987). In this extract Nevo argues that *The Taming of the Shrew* is a "psychodrama."]

All of Padua, we are given to understand, is taken up with the problem of finding someone to take his devilish daughter off Baptista's hands, leaving the field free for the suitors of the heavenly Bianca. And this is precisely a trap in which Kate is caught. She has become nothing but an obstacle or a means to her sister's advancement. Even the husband they seek for her is in reality for the sister's sake, not hers. When she says: 'I will never marry' it is surely because she believes no 'real' husband of her own, who loves her for herself, whom she can trust, is possible. How indeed could it be otherwise since patently and manifestly no one does love her? Because (or therefore) she is not lovable. And the more unlovable she is the more she proves her point. Katherina of Acts I and II is a masterly and familiar portrait. No one about her can do right in her eyes, so great is her envy and suspicion. No one can penetrate her defences, so great her need for assurance. So determined is she to make herself invulnerable that she makes herself insufferable, and finds in insufferability her one defence. This is a 'knot of errors' of formidable proportions and will require no less than Petruchio's shock tactics for its undoing.

The undoing begins with the arrival of Petruchio, to wive it wealthily in Padua. No doubts are entertained in Padua about the benefits of marriage where money is, but it will be noted that no one is banking on a rich marriage to save him from the bankruptcy courts. All the suitors are wealthy; Lucentio, potentially at least. The contrast that Shakespeare sets up between Petruchio and Lucentio is an interesting ironic inversion of that obtaining in the Terentian tradition. In Terence the second (liaison) plot entailed tricky stratagems for acquiring money in order to buy (and keep) the slave girl. The main (marriage) plot on the other hand hinged upon the fortunate discovery of a true identity, which meant both legitimizing the affair and acquiring the dowry. Here, in the case of Bianca and Lucentio the mercenary mechanics of match-making are masked by Petrarchan ardours on Lucentio's part (or Hortensio's, until the appearance of the widow):

> Tranio, I burn, I pine, I perish, Tranio,
>
> . . . let me be a slave, t'achieve that maid
> Whose sudden sight hath thrall'd my wounded eye.
> (I.i.155; 219–20)

and by angelic docility on Bianca's part; while Petruchio's affairs are deromanticized by the unabashed, unmasked worldiness of his motivation:

> I come to wive it wealthily in Padua;
> If wealthily, then happily in Padua.
> (I.ii.75–6)

and the formidable temper of Kate. 〈 . . . 〉

In *The Shrew,* Shakespeare's characteristic handling of multiple levels is already to be discerned. The main protagonists are the agents of the higher recognitions, the middle groups function as screens on which are projected distorted mirror images of the main couples—images in a concave mirror; while the lower orders ridicule the middle by the parody of imitation, and act as foils for the higher by providing a measure of qualitative difference.

Though *The Shrew* fails to integrate Christopher Sly satisfactorily and indeed abandons him altogether after Act I, such a function for him, as I have already indicated, is adumbrated. Shakespeare, it seems, felt more comfortable with the playlet-within-the-play of *Love's Labour's Lost* and *A Midsummer Night's Dream* for his clowns, or with the parenthetic internal comment of a cunning and a foolish servant combination like Grumio/Tranio or Launce/Speed than with the clown-frame, to which he does not return. But the flurry of disguisings and contrivings, 'supposes' and role-playings in Baptista's middle-class household, resolved finally by nothing more complex than natural selection and substantial bank balances, do set off admirably the subtler, more complex and interiorized transformations of the Petruchio-Katherina relationship.

—Ruth Nevo, *Comic Transformation in Shakespeare* (London: Methuen, 1980): pp. 41–43.

JOEL FINEMAN ON THE TURN OF THE SHREW

[Joel Fineman is a professor at the University of California, Berkeley. He is the author of *Shakespeare's Perjured Eye: The Invention of Poetic Subjectivity in the Sonnets* and of essays on Shakespeare and on literary theory. This essay is taken from *Shakespeare and the Question of Theory* (1985). Here Fineman analyzes Kate's feminine and Petruchio's more masculine language.]

In ways which are so traditional that they might be called proverbial, Shakespeare's *Taming of the Shrew* assumes—it turns out to make no difference whether it does so ironically—that the language of woman is at odds with the order and authority of man. At the same time, again in ways which are nothing but traditional, the play self-consciously associates this thematically subversive discourse of woman with its own literariness and theatricality. The result, however, is a play that speaks neither for the language of woman nor against the authority of man. Quite the contrary: at the end of the play things are pretty much the same—which is to say, patriarchally inflected—as they were at or before its beginning, the only difference being that now, because there are more shrews than ever, they are more so. It cannot be surprising that a major and perennially popular play by Shakespeare, which is part of a corpus that, at least in an English literary tradition, is synonymous with what is understood to be canonical, begins and ends as something orthodox. Nevertheless, there is reason to wonder—as my epigraph, the last lines of the play, suggests—how it happens that a discourse of subversion, explicitly presented as such, manages to resecure, equally explicitly, the very order to which it seems, at both first and second sight, to be opposed. This question, raised by the play in a thematic register, and posed practically by the play by virtue of the play's historical success, leads to another: is it possible to voice a language, whether of man or of woman, that does not speak, sooner or later, self-consciously or unconsciously, for the order and authority of man?

Formulated at considerably greater levels of generality, such questions have been advanced by much recent literary, and not only literary, theory, much of which finds it very difficult to sustain in any intelligible fashion an effective critical and adversary distance or difference between itself and any of a variety of master points of view, each of which claims special access to a global, universalizing truth. It is, however, in the debates and polemics growing out of and centering upon the imperial claims of psychoanalysis that such questions have been raised in the very same terms and at precisely the level of generality proposed by *The Taming of the Shrew*—the level of generality measured by the specificity of rubrics as massive and as allegorically suggestive as Man, Woman, and Language—for it is psychoanalysis, especially the psychoanalysis associated with the name of Jacques Lacan, that has most coherently developed an account of human subjectivity which is based upon the fact that human beings speak. Very much taking this speech to heart, psychoanalysis has organized, in much the same ways as does *The Taming of the Shrew,* the relationship of generic Man to generic Woman by reference to the apparently inescapable patriarchalism occasioned by the structuring effects of language—of Language, that is to say, which is also understood in broad genericizing terms. In turn, the most forceful criticisms of psychoanalysis, responding to the psychoanalytic provocation with a proverbial response, have all been obliged, again repeating the thematics of *The Taming of the Shrew*, to speak against this Language for which the psychoanalytic speaks.

—Joel Fineman, "The Turn of the Shrew," in *Shakespeare and the Question of Theory,* ed. Patricia Parker and Geoffrey Hartman (London: Methuen, 1985). Reprinted in *William Shakespeare's The Taming of the Shrew,* ed. Harold Bloom (New York: Chelsea House, 1988): pp. 93–94.

Plot Summary of
A Midsummer Night's Dream

The period 1595–96 is usually accepted as the date of composition of *A Midsummer Night's Dream.* Critics agree that this drama shares stylistic affinities with *Richard II* and *Romeo and Juliet.* The influence of Ovid's *Metamorphoses* and Chaucer's *Knight's Tale* are evident in this comedy. Also, Bottom's transformation may be owed to Apuleus' *Golden Ass,* a work available in translation in Shakespeare's time. Regardless of the sources, Shakespeare in this play succeeds in synthesizing different places and times and different literary traditions into a united dramatic whole. A visionary play with its unusual variety of meters, verse forms, and the lunar spirit that dominates the play, *A Midsummer Night's Dream* explores the capriciousness and changeability of love.

Act I, scene one opens in Athens, with a scene between Theseus, the Duke of Athens and Hippolyta, Queen of the Amazons, who are to be married at the next new moon, in four days. Theseus orders Philostate, his master of the revels, to "stir up the Athenians youths to merriment." Egeus enters with his daughter, Hermia, and Lysander and Demetrius, her two suitors. Hermia loves Lysander but is also loved by Demetrius, who has her father's permission to marry her. Since Hermia refuses to obey her father's wish, the case is brought to Theseus. Egeus has Theseus' full support and Hermia is given two options: "either to die the death, or to abjure forever the society of men." The two suitors assert themselves in this scene: Demetrius asks Hermia to yield to her father's choice, whereas Lysander proposes that Egeus and Demetrius should marry considering how much they love each other. He also remarks that Demetrius has no constant heart as a lover; not that long ago he wooed Helena, Hermia's best friend. In order to escape the Athenian law, Lysander and Hermia secretly plot to flee Athens and take refuge with Lysander's aunt where they can get married. Lysander, nevertheless, reveals their plan to Helena, who plans tell Demetrius, hoping that this will help her gain back his love. All four characters are slightly individualized and subordinated to the pattern of the play.

In **Act I,** scene two the comic subplot begins at Quince the carpenter's house, where a group of artisans plan to present a play, *The Most Lam-*

entable Comedy and Most Cruel Death of Pyramus and Thisby, a tragic love story quite inappropriate for the nuptial celebration of Theseus and Hippolyta. The part of Pyramus is assigned to Nick Bottom, the weaver; Thisby to Francis Flute, the bellows-mender; Robin Starveling, the tailor, will play Thisby's mother; Tom Snout, the tinker, will act as Pyramus' father; Quince will take the role of Thisby's father; and Sung, the joiner, the Lion's part. Quince asks the troupe to meet for rehearsal in a wood the next night. Shakespeare introduces each man's personality while they are choosing their roles.

The world of the fairies (which will intervene in the activities of the characters) is introduced in **Act II**, scene one. Fairies, invisible to the other characters (only Bottom is given the privilege of seeing Titania) live in the wood in which Lysander and Hermia agree to meet, as does the troupe of artisans. Puck, a mischievous fellow (the word *puck* or Old English *pouke* means a demon) who descends from Robin Goodfellow or Hobgoblin, reveals that his master, Oberon, King of Fairies, is quarreling with Titania, his Queen, over "a little changeling boy." Even though they are ethereal beings, Oberon and Titania have human emotions: they enter onto the stage, quarrel, and are torn apart by jealousy. To punish the Queen for keeping the child whom he wants to be his henchman, Oberon orders Puck to fetch a flower with the fancy name "love-in-idleness" (pansy), whose juice squeezed and placed on the sleeping eyelids will make the man or woman fall in love with the first being he or she sees upon waking. With this design in his mind, he plans to drop the liquor on the eyes of Titania and stir passion in her heart for some unworthy being ("Be it on lion, bear, or wolf, or bull/on meddling monkey, or on busy ape" [II, i, 184–5].) He will not lift the spell until she gives him the boy. Upon hearing others approaching Oberon makes himself invisible. Demetrius, pursued by Helena, is searching for Lysander and Hermia. He wishes to kill Lysander and is very harsh in his treatment of Helena. Oberon witnesses Demetrius' abandonment of Helena, and, when Puck returns with the magic flower, he orders that besides anointing Titania's eyes, Puck should use some of the juice on the eyes of a "disdainful youth" in Athenian garment. He is not, however, aware that there are two such youths in the wood.

In **Act II,** scene two as soon as Titania has fallen asleep, Oberon steals in and sprinkles her eyes with the flower juice. Puck approaches Lysander and Hermia, who have fallen asleep near Titania's flowery bed. He takes Lysander to be the "youth in Athenian garment" and pours some juice onto his eyes. At this point Helena enters chasing Demetrius, who runs off. Helena wakes up Lysander, not knowing whether he is dead or asleep. The charm works, but not as designed: Lysander falls in love with Helena, who, at his declarations of love, thinks she is being mocked. Lysander chases Helena into the wood, whereas Hermia, upon awaking, finds herself alone and begins to search for Lysander.

Act III begins with the artisans who meet in the wood to rehearse their play. They choose a spot next to the sleeping Titania. Puck transforms Bottom by putting an ass's head on his shoulder. The rest of the artisans flee, but Bottom, unaware of his altered state, walks up and down, cheerfully singing. The song wakens Titania, who instantaneously declares her love to Bottom, as an aftereffect of the magic flower juice. Bottom, a little perplexed, responds: "Methinks, mistress, you should have little reason for that. And yet, to say the truth, reason and love keep little company together nowadays" (III, i, 136–8). Bottom has captured with these words one of the themes of the play. Titania displays her love with verses: "I am a spirit of no common rate;/The summer still doth tend upon my state;/And I do love thee: therefore go with me (III, i, 147–9). She summons her elves Peaseblossom, Cobweb, Moth, and Mustardseed to attend Bottom.

In another part of the wood, (**Act III,** scene two) Puck recounts recent events to Oberon. Oberon realizes that Puck has put the magic juice on the wrong youth. He sends Puck to find Helena and bring her back to the sleeping Demetrius, while he uses the magic flower-juice on his eyes. Helena enters, followed by the pursuing Lysander, who continues to vow his love for her. Demetrius wakens and now he, too, falls instantly in love with Helena. At the beginning of the play both men loved Hermia; here, with the subtle development of the plot, we see both men now competing to prove who is more truly in love with Helena. (Did Shakespeare want to show the arbitrariness of romantic love?) Hermia then reappears, bewildered by the new situation. Helena, alas, thinks that all three of them are conspiring to make fun of her. Puck leads Lysander and Demetrius away; Oberon, trying again to set matter straight, sends Puck to find an antidote to his "love-in-idleness," which will restore Lysander's love for Hermia.

By the end of **Act IV** all the affairs are resolved. In scene one Oberon and Puck find Titania asleep with the ass-headed Bottom in her arms. Oberon, having made sure that he has the changeling boy, releases Titania from the charm, and Titania wakens with a shadowy remembrance of her enchantment. Oberon also commands Puck to remove the ass's head from Bottom, and Titania reconciles with Oberon.

Theseus, Hippolyta, and Egeus enter into the wood planning to go hunting. They come across the four lovers mysteriously sleeping. Egeus recognizes them and, upon questioning, finds out that Demetrius is now in love with Helena and that he has no claims on Hermia. They pair off happily: Hermia with Lysander, and Helena with Demetrius. The Duke is pleased and he invites the lovers to be married at the same time as his own marriage.

The last of the dreamers, Nick Bottom, left alone on the stage, awakens, vaguely remembering his adventures, only certain that he had "a most rare vision," about which he plans to write a ballet (ballad), cleverly called "Bottom's Dream" because, as he states, it has no bottom.

Act IV, scene two shows Bottom's friends alarmed over his disappearance. Bottom makes an entrance and momentarily takes charge of the performance of the play.

In **Act V,** Shakespeare presents the play of Pyramus and Thesbe. We find Theseus and Hippolyta in the middle of a conversation about the strange things "these lovers speak of." Theseus utters memorable lines comparing the madman, the lover, and the poet: "Lovers and madmen have such seething brains,/Such shaping fantasies, that apprehend/ more than cool reason ever comprehends./The lunatic, the lover, and the poet/Are of imagination all compact" (V, i, 4–8). The craftsmen perform the "most lamentable comedy" of Pyramus and Thisby (the play-within-the-play) and the audience laughs at its ineptitudes. The execution of the tragic play is a success. Theseus dismisses the actors and asks the lovers to go to bed. Theseus' couplet, "A fortnight hold we this solemnity,/In nightly revels and new jollity" can be taken as the end of the play. Shakespeare, however, prolongs the play in order to present once again the world of the fairies. Only with Puck's closing verses is the line between illusion and reality confirmed. ❀

List of Characters in
A Midsummer Night's Dream

Theseus, Duke of Athens, is presented as a wise ruler. He is in love with Hippolyta, whose land he has conquered in recent battle, and to whom he is engaged to be married. His word is respected by other characters in the play, and he appears as arbitrator in the love dispute.

Hippolyta, the Queen of Amazons, is betrothed to Theseus. She plays a small part in the drama.

Egeus is Hermia's father, who insists that she marry Demetrius instead of the man she loves, Lysander.

Hermia, daughter of Egeus, is in love with Lysander. Her father wants her to marry Demetrius, however. When she asserts her choice to Theseus, he proclaims she must yield to her father's will or go to a nunnery. Showing "a mind of her own," she flees with Lysander to the woods. She marries Lysander at the end of the play.

Helena, Hermia's best friend, is in love with Demetrius. Described as tall and blonde, she is physically contrasted to Hermia, who is a short brunette. Helena is also represented as less spirited than Hermia. She discloses to Demetrius Lysander's and Hermia's plan to flee to the forest. She marries Demetrius at the end of the play.

Lysander is Hermia's beloved. When Puck mistakenly anoints magic flower-juice onto his eyes, he falls in love with Helena. Finally, after an antidote is applied, he marries Hermia.

Demetrius is in love with Hermia and has her father's approval to get married. Because he wooed Helena before Hermia, Lysander accuses him of not having a constant heart. In the woods, under the spell of the love-juice, he falls in love with Helena again, and at last marries her.

Oberon is the king of the Fairies, a spirit with human emotions. He orders Puck to fetch the magical flower "love-in-idleness" and put its juice on Titania's eyelids as well as on a "disdainful youth in Athenian garment" so that she will fall in love with the first being upon awaking. That being happens to be Bottom, the weaver. Oberon is omnipresent in the play but still knows less than the audience.

Titania is the Queen of the Fairies. She doesn't want to give to Oberon "a little changeling boy." When she awakes after the magical juice has been put on her eyes, she falls in love with Nick Bottom. Nevertheless, she and Oberon settle and she gives up the boy.

Puck, a descendant of Robin Goodfellow or Hobgoblin, thinks all mortals are fools. He is a spirit who can move at incredible speed. He is also the link between the world of mortals and immortals. He closes the play by tidying the stage with the broom.

Peaseblossom, Cobweb, Moth, and **Mustardseed** are Queen Titania's elves, who serve as attendants upon Nick Bottom, on the command of their Queen, Titania.

Nick Bottom, a weaver, decides to put on a play about Pyramus and Thisby for Theseus' wedding. His transformation into a creature with an ass's head doesn't confuse him at all. Queen Titania falls in love with him and he sleeps in her arms. When the spell is broken, he only vaguely remembers what happened to him.

Quince, Flute, Snug, Starveling, and **Snout** are the craftsmen who, together with Bottom, present the "lamentable comedy" before the Duke for his wedding. ❀

Critical Views on
A Midsummer Night's Dream

SAMUEL TAYLOR COLERIDGE ON HELENA'S BETRAYAL

[Samuel Taylor Coleridge (1772–1834), aside from being one of the greatest British poets of the early nineteenth century, was also a penetrating critic. His most famous critical work is *Biographia Literaria* (1817). In 1819 he delivered a series of lectures on Shakespeare, which were published posthumously in his *Literary Remains* (1836–1839). When additional lecture material was found, Coleridge's lectures were republished in the two-volume *Shakespearean Criticism* (1930). In this extract he analyzes Helena's betrayal of Hermia to Demetrius.]

In Act 1, Scene I Helena betrays Hermia to Demetrius:

> I will go tell him of fair Hermia's flight.
> (I.i.246.)

I am convinced that Shakespeare availed himself of the title of the play in his own mind [as] a *dream* throughout, but especially (and perhaps unpleasingly) in this broad determination of ungrateful treachery in Helena, so undisguisedly avowed to herself, and this too after the witty cool philosophizing that precedes. The act is very natural; the resolve so to act is, I fear, likewise too true a picture of the lax hold that principles have on the female heart, when opposed to, or even separated from, passion and inclination. For women are less hypocrites to their own minds than men, because they feel less abhorrence of moral evil in itself and more for its outward consequences, as detection, loss of character, etc., their natures being almost wholly extroitive. But still, however just, the representation is not poetical; we shrink from it and cannot harmonize it with the ideal.

—Samuel Taylor Coleridge, *Shakespearean Criticism*, ed. T. M. Raysor (London: J. M. Dent & Sons Ltd., 1930): p. 90.

G. K. Chesterton on Shakespeare's Mysticism of Happiness

[G. K. Chesterton (1874–1936) was a British critic and author of verse, essays, novels, and short stories, known also for his exuberant personality. Among his works of literary criticism are monographs on Robert Browning (1903), Charles Dickens (1906), George Bernard Shaw (1909), William Blake (1910), and Geoffrey Chaucer (1910). In this extract, Chesterton praises *Dream* for its "mysticism of happiness."]

Now in the reason for this modern and pedantic error lies the whole secret and difficulty of such plays as *A Midsummer Night's Dream*. The sentiment of such a play, so far as it can be summed up at all, can be summed up in one sentence. It is the mysticism of happiness. That is to say, it is the conception that as man lives upon a borderland he may find himself in the spiritual or supernatural atmosphere, not only through being profoundly sad or meditative, but by being extravagantly happy. The soul might be rapt out of the body in an agony of sorrow, or a trance of ecstasy; but it might also be rapt out of the body in a paroxysm of laughter. Sorrow we know can go beyond itself; so, according to Shakespeare, can pleasure go beyond itself and become something dangerous and unknown. And the reason that the logical and destructive modern school, of which Mr. Bernard Shaw is an example, does not grasp this purely exuberant nature of the comedies is simply that their logical and destructive attitude have rendered impossible the very experience of this preternatural exuberance. We cannot realize *As You Like It* if we are always considering it as we understand it. We cannot have *A Midsummer Night's Dream* if our one object in life is to keep ourselves awake with the black coffee of criticism. The whole question which is balanced, and balanced nobly and fairly, in *A Midsummer Night's Dream,* is whether the life of waking, or the life of the vision, is the real life, the *sine quâ non* of man. But it is difficult to see what superiority for the purpose of judging is possessed by people whose pride it is not to live the life of vision at all. At least it is questionable whether the Elizabethan did not know more about both worlds than the modern intellectual; it is not altogether improbable that Shakespeare would not only have had a clearer vision of the fairies, but would have shot very much straighter at a deer and netted much more money for his performances than a member of the Stage Society.

In pure poetry and the intoxication of words, Shakespeare never rose higher than he rises in this play. But in spite of this fact the supreme literary merit of *A Midsummer Night's Dream* is a merit of design. The amazing symmetry, the amazing artistic and moral beauty of that design, can be stated very briefly. The story opens in the sane and common world with the pleasant seriousness of very young lovers and very young friends. Then, as the figures advance into the tangled wood of young troubles and stolen happiness, a change and bewilderment begins to fall on them. They lose their way and their wits for they are in the heart of fairyland. Their words, their hungers, their very figures grow more and more dim and fantastic, like dreams within dreams, in the supernatural mist of Puck. Then the dream-fumes begin to clear, and characters and spectators begin to awaken together to the noise of horns and dogs and the clean and bracing morning. Theseus, the incarnation of a happy and generous rationalism, expounds in hackneyed and superb lines the sane view of such psychic experiences, pointing out with a reverent and sympathetic scepticism that all these fairies and spells are themselves but the emanations, the unconscious masterpieces, of man himself. The whole company falls back into a splendid human laughter. There is a rush for banqueting and private theatricals, and over all these things ripples one of those frivolous and inspired conversations in which every good saying seems to die in giving birth to another. If ever the son of man in his wanderings was at home and drinking by the fireside, he is at home in the house of Theseus. All the dreams have been forgotten, as a melancholy dream remembered throughout the morning might be forgotten in the human certainty of any other triumphant evening party; and so the play seems naturally ended. It began on the earth and it ends on the earth. Thus to round off the whole midsummer night's dream in an eclipse of daylight is an effect of genius. But of this comedy, as I have said, the mark is that genius goes beyond itself; and one touch is added which makes the play colossal. Theseus and his train retire with a crashing finale, full of humour and wisdom and things set right, and silence falls on the house. Then there comes a faint sound of little feet, and for a moment, as it were, the elves look into the house, asking which is the reality. "Suppose we are the realities and they the shadows." If that ending were acted properly any modern man would feel shaken to his marrow if he had to walk home from the theatre through a country lane.

—G. K. Chesterton, *Chesterton on Shakespeare,* ed. Dorothy Collins (Henley-on-Thames: Darwin Finlayson, 1936): pp. 104–106.

G. Wilson Knight on Imagery and Fairyland

[G. Wilson Knight (1897–1985), a leading British Shakespeare scholar, taught drama and English literature at the University of Leeds. He was the author of many volumes of criticism, including *The Starlit Dome* (1941), *The Crown of Life* (1947), and *Shakespeare and Religion* (1967). In this extract from *The Shakespearean Tempest* (1932), Knight asserts that there is a *Macbeth*-like quality to the fairy world and the moonlight imagery.]

In this play fairyland interpenetrates the world of human action. And that world is varied, ranging from the rough simplicity of the clowns, through the solid common sense and kind worldly wisdom of Theseus, to the frenzied fantasies of the lovers: which in their turn shade into fairyland itself. The play thus encloses remarkably a whole scale of intuitions. Nor in any other early romance is the interplay of imagery more exquisitely varied. The night is a-glimmer with moon and star, yet it is dark and fearsome; there are gentle birds and gruesome beasts. There is a gnomish, fearsome, *Macbeth*-like quality about the atmosphere, just touching nightmare: yet these fairies are the actualization of Shakespeare's Indian dream. The total result resembles those dreams, of substance unhappy to the memorizing intellect, which yet, on waking, we find ourselves strangely regretting, loath to part from that magic even when it leaves nothing to the memory but incidents which should be painful. Such are the fairies here. They are neither good nor bad. They are wayward spirits which cause trouble to men, yet also woo human love and favour: as when Oberon and Titanis quarrel for their Indian boy or wrangle in jealousy of Theseus or Hippolyta. The whole vision sums and expresses, as does no other work, the magic and the mystery of sleep, the dewy sweetness of a midsummer dream, dawn-memoried with sparkling grass and wreathing mists; a morning slope falling from a glade where late the moonbeams glimmered their fairy light on shadowed mossy boles and fearsome dells, and the vast woodland silence.

The action depends largely on Oberon's quarrel with Titania. Dissension has entered fairyland itself, due to these spirits' desire for human love, just as later human beings are caused trouble by their contact with the fairies:

> Why art thou here,
> Come from the farthest steppe of India?

But that, forsooth, the bouncing Amazon,
Your buskin'd mistress and your warrior love,
To Theseus must be wedded, and you come
To give their bed joy and prosperity.

(II.i.68)

Oberon parries Titania's speech with reciprocal jealousy. Now this dissension makes 'tempests' in nature, untuning the melodic procession of the seasons. ⟨ . . . ⟩

The play continually suggests a nightmare terror. It is dark and fearsome. The nights here are 'grim-look'd' (V.i.171). And yet this atmosphere of gloom and dread is the playground for the purest comedy. Romance and fun interthread our tragedies here. So, too, a pale light falls from moon and star into the darkened glades, carving the trees into deeper darkness, black voiceless giants; yet silvering the mossy slopes; lighting the grass with misty sparkles of flame; setting green fire to the glimmering eyes of prowling beasts; dissolving Oberon and Puck invisible in their magic beams.

The play is full of moonlight. The opening lines are a fine introduction:

THESEUS: Now, fair Hippolyta, our nuptial hour
Draws on apace; four happy days bring in
Another moon: but, O, methinks how slow
The old moon wanes! She lingers my desires
Like to a step-dame or a dowager
Long withering out a young man's revenue.
HIPPOLYTA: Four days will quickly steep themselves in night;
Four nights will quickly dream away the time;
And then the moon, like to a silver bow
New bent in heaven, shall behold the night
Of our solemnities.

(I.i.1)

Egeus accuses Lysander of singing love verses 'by moonlight' to Hermia (I.i.30); and Theseus images nuns as 'chanting faint hymns to the cold fruitless moon' (I.i.73); both these associating moonlight with music. Hermia is to reach her decision 'by the next new moon' (I.i.83). Then Lysander plots his and her escape, and tells Helena, using a lovely 'moon' image:

To-morrow night, when Phebe doth behold
Her silver visage in the watery glass,
Decking with liquid pearl the bladed grass . . .

(I.i.209)

A fine association of the moon, smooth waters, and jewel-imagery. Titania's fairy wanders 'swifter than the moon's sphere' (II.i.7). In Titania's tempest-speech, no night is 'with hymn or carol blest' and therefore the moon, 'governess of floods', is 'pale' with anger, and washes the air with rheumatic dampness (II.i.102). Another association of the moon with votive song. Oberon tells how he saw Cupid flying 'between the cold moon and the earth' (II.i.156), and how this arrow was 'quench'd in the chaste beams of the watery moon' (II.i.162). Titania would have her elves 'fan the moonbeams' from Bottom's 'sleeping eyes' (III.i.176), and shortly after speaks these lines:

> The moon, methinks, looks with a watery eye;
> And, when she weeps, weeps every little flower,
> Lamenting some enforced chastity.
>
> (III.i.203)

—G. Wilson Knight, *The Shakespearean Tempest* (London: Methuen, 1932, 1960): 142–143, 146–147.

Northrop Frye on Expounding the Dream

[Northrop Frye (1912–1991), formerly a professor of English at Victoria University in Toronto, was a highly respected literary critic. Among his works are *Anatomy of Criticism* (1957), *A Natural Perspective: The Development of Shakespearean Comedy and Romance* (1965), and *Fools of Time* (1967), a study of Shakespeare's tragedies. *The Great Code: The Bible and Literature,* a study of the mythology and structure of the Bible, was published in 1982. In this extract (taken from *Frye on Shakespeare*) Frye studies the title of the play and Bottom's ballad.]

Why is this play called *A Midsummer Night's Dream?* Apparently the main action in the fairy wood takes place on the eve of May Day; at any rate, when Theseus and Hippolyta enter with the rising sun, they discover the four lovers, and Theseus says:

> No doubt they rose up early to observe
> The rite of May.
>
> (4.1.131–32)

We call the time of the summer solstice, in the third week of June, "mid-summer," although in our calendars it's the beginning of summer. That's because originally there were only three seasons, summer, autumn and winter: summer then included spring and began in March. A thirteenth-century song begins "sumer is i-cumen in," generally modernized, to keep the metre, as "summer is a-coming in," but it doesn't mean that: it means "spring is here." The Christian calendar finally established the celebration of the birth of Christ at the winter solstice, and made a summer solstice date (June 24) the feast day of John the Baptist. This arrangement, according to the Fathers, symbolized John's remark in the Gospels on beholding Christ: "He must increase, but I must decrease." Christmas Eve was a beneficent time, when evil spirits had no power; St. John's Eve was perhaps more ambiguous, and there was a common phrase, "midsummer madness," used by Olivia in *Twelfth Night*, a play named after the opposite end of the year. Still, it was a time when spirits of nature, whether benevolent or malignant, might be supposed to be abroad.

There were also two other haunted "eves," of the first of November and of the first of May. These take us back to a still earlier time, when animals were brought in from the pasture at the beginning of winter, with a slaughter of those that couldn't be kept to feed, and when they were let out again at the beginning of spring. The first of these survives in our Hallowe'en, but May Day eve is no longer thought of much as a spooky time, although in Germany, where it was called "Walpurgis night," the tradition that witches held an assembly on a mountain at that time lasted much longer, and comes into Goethe's *Faust*. In *Faust* the scene with the witches is followed by something called "The Golden Wedding of Oberon and Titania," which has nothing to do with Shakespeare's play, but perhaps indicates a connection in Goethe's mind between it and the first of May.

In Shakespeare's time, as Theseus's remark indicates, the main emphasis on the first of May fell on a sunrise service greeting the day with songs. All the emphasis was on hope and cheerfulness. Shakespeare evidently doesn't want to force a specific date on us: it may be May Day eve, but all we can be sure of is that it's later than St. Valentine's Day in mid-February, the day when traditionally the birds start copulating, and we could have guessed that anyway. The general idea is that we have gone through the kind of night when spirits are powerful but not necessarily malevolent. Evil spirits, as we learn from the opening scene of *Hamlet*, are forced to disappear at dawn, and the fact that this is also true of the Ghost of Hamlet's father sows a terrible doubt in Hamlet's mind. Here we have Puck, or more accurately Robin Goodfellow *the* puck. Pucks were a category of spirits who were often sinister, and the Puck of this play is clearly mischievous. But we are expressly told by Oberon that the fairies of whom he's the king are "spirits of another sort," not evil and not restricted to darkness.

So the title of the play simply emphasizes the difference between the two worlds of the action, the waking world of Theseus's court and the fairy world of Oberon. ⟨ . . . ⟩

Which brings me to Bottom, the only mortal in the play who actually sees any of the fairies. One of the last things Bottom says in the play is rather puzzling: "the wall is down that parted their fathers." Apparently he means the wall separating the hostile families of Pyramus and Thisbe. This wall seems to have attracted attention: after Snout the tinker, taking the part of Wall, leaves the stage, Theseus says, according to the Folio: "Now is the morall downe between the two neighbours." The New Arden editor reads "mural down," and other editors simply change to "wall down." The Quarto, just to be helpful, reads "moon used." Wall and Moonshine between them certainly confuse an already confused play. One wonders if the wall between the two worlds of Theseus and Oberon, the wall that Theseus is so sure is firmly in place, doesn't throw a shadow on these remarks.

Anyway, Bottom wakes up along with the lovers and makes one of the most extraordinary speeches in Shakespeare, which includes a very scrambled but still recognizable echo from the New Testament, and finally says he will get Peter Quince to write a ballad of his dream, and "it shall be called Bottom's Dream, because it hath no bottom." Like most of what Bottom says, this is absurd; like many absurdities in Shakespeare, it makes a lot of sense. Bottom does not know that he is anticipating by three centuries a remark of Freud: "every dream has a point at which it is unfathomable; a link, as it were, with the unknown." When we come to *King Lear*, we shall suspect that it takes a madman to see into the heart of a tragedy, and perhaps it takes a fool or clown, who habitually breathes the atmosphere of absurdity and paradox, to see into the heart of comedy. "Man," says Bottom, "is but an ass, if he go about to expound this dream." But it was Bottom the ass who had the dream, not Bottom the weaver, who is already forgetting it. He will never see his Titania again, not even remember that she had once loved him, or doted on him, to use Friar Laurence's distinction. But he has been closer to the centre of this wonderful and mysterious play than any other of its characters, and it no longer matters that Puck thinks him a fool or that Titania loathes his asinine face.

—Northrop Frye, *Northrop Frye on Shakespeare* ed. Robert Sandler (New Haven: Yale University Press, 1986). Reprinted in *William Shakespeare's A Midsummer Night's Dream*, ed. Harold Bloom (New York: Chelsea House, 1987): pp. 124–125, 131–132.

E. Talbot Donaldson on Shakespeare Reading Chaucer

[E. Talbot Donaldson, Professor Emeritus of English at Indiana University at Bloomington, taught also at Yale, Columbia, and London University. Among his books are *Piers Plowman: The C-Text and Its Poet; Chaucer's Poetry: An Anthology for Modern Reader* (2nd edition, 1975) which serves as the standard for modern Chaucer scholarship and criticism; *Speaking of Chaucer* (1983), and *The Swan at the Well: Shakespeare Reading Chaucer* (1985). Here Donaldson compares Theseus in *A Knight's Tale* and in *A Midsummer Night's Dream;* and a love-hate motif in lovers.]

The most fully responsible character in Chaucer's *Knight's Tale* and in *A Midsummer Night's Dream* is Theseus, Duke of Athens. But while this mentor-figure is often said to be the only character that Shakespeare adopted from Chaucer without change, the second Theseus seems to me somewhat less mature, less philosophical, and a good deal more skeptical than the first. Both Theseuses are, it is true, experienced, orderly, tolerant men who show becoming sympathy for the idiotic behavior of a parcel of young lovers in the woods, whether the woods are of fourteenth-century Athens-on-Thames or sixteenth-century Athens-on-Avon. But the second Theseus draws as much from Chaucer's Knight as he does from the Knight's Theseus, especially in his reluctance to speculate about matters beyond his ken. Chaucer's Knight, after giving a remorselessly harrowing account of Arcite's death, informs us, with a lightness of spirit that some find shocking, that Arcite's spirit went somewhere, but where he knows not, not having been there himself and being no theologian. The Knight's Theseus, on the other hand, has more assurance in such matters, and in his final speech in the poem speaks of mourning for Arcite's death as folly, because Arcite has escaped from "the foul prison of this life." He does not, of course, pinpoint

Arcite's final destination, but it seems to be a better place than here, for his speech is an attempt to establish the existence of a divine plan behind the randomness that has controlled the events of *The Knight's Tale*. But Shakespeare's Theseus shares the Knight's skepticism about what he has not seen with his own eyes. Hippolyta's remark about the lovers' confused story of their enchanted night in the woods, " 'Tis strange, my Theseus, that these lover speak of," evokes from him the unillusioned reply,

> More strange than true. I never may believe
> These antique fables, not these fairy toys.
> (V.i.2–3)

⟨ . . . ⟩ While Lysander and Demetrius love as intensely as Palamon and Arcite, the intensity of their hatred for one another is, if possible, even greater than that of their forebears. Comparatively speaking, Palamon and Arcite seem to wish to slay one another in the interests of a higher principle, as it were, and so without rancor. But Demetrius boasts that he is out to slaughter Lysander when he first follows his rival and Hermia into the woods, and once Lysander has received an application of Love-in-Idleness and wakes to erupt in love with Helena, his hatred for Demetrius explodes simultaneously. After announcing his love for Helena in three lines, he adds,

> Where is Demetrius? O how fit a word
> Is that vile name to perish on my sword!
> (II.ii.105–06)

If we consider that at this time he presumably knows that Demetrius does not love Helena, then we must conclude that he hates him not as a rival but as one who has insulted his own new love by not loving her. But perhaps such a superabundance of hatred needs no reason. Subsequently, after Demetrius has received his application of essence-of-pansy and wakes to love Helena again, the two men become as occupied with killing one another as they are in making love to their bewildered mistress. They are prevented from mutual slaughter only by Helena's physical intervention, and later by Puck's keeping them apart as they pursue each other through the woods.

But Shakespeare has added a new dimension as well as new intensity to the love-hate motif. The monomania of the lovers also expresses itself in the vehement loathing they both feel for the woman they just now loved passionately, as if an emotionally neutral state were impossible to them. When Helena follows Demetrius into the woods, his gentlemanly instincts yield instantly to revulsion. He begins patiently by telling her, "I love thee not, therefore pursue me not," but when that has no effect, he inquires sarcastically whether he is not telling her in plainest truth that he does not nor cannot love her. And when that does not dissuade her from following, he tells her

> Tempt not too much hatred of my spirit;
> For I am sick when I do look on thee.
>   (II.i.211–12)

After Lysander wakes to love Helena and vows to kill Demetrius, he addresses the still sleeping Hermia thus:

> Hermia, sleep thou there,
> And never mayst thou come Lysander near!
> For, as a surfeit of the sweetest things
> The deepest loathing to the stomach brings;
> Or as the heresies that men do leave
> Are hatred most of those they did not deceive;
> So thou, my surfeit and my heresy,
> Of all be hated, but the most of me!
>   (II.ii.134–41)

After this blessing in reverse, he leaves her to face alone the universal hatred he has called down upon her. Titania, released by Dian's bud from the effects of Love-in-Idleness, looks upon her former beloved, the sleeping Bottom, and exclaims, "O how mine eyes do loathe his visage now!" (IV.i.78) Lysander and Demetrius could not be more hateful to their former loves if both the ladies had sprouted ass's heads.

—E. Talbot Donaldson, *The Swan at the Well: Shakespeare Reading Chaucer* (New Haven: Yale University Press, 1985): pp. 32–33, 38–39.

HAROLD BLOOM ON BOTTOM'S COMMON SENSE AND NATURAL GOODNESS

[Harold Bloom is Sterling Professor of the Humanities at Yale University and Berg Professor of English at New York University. He is the author of more than 20 books, including an important new study of William Shakespeare, *Shakespeare, the Invention of the Human* (1998), and the editor of over 40 anthologies and works of literary criticism. In this extract, taken from his Introduction to *A Midsummer Night's Dream* in the Chelsea House series MODERN CRITICAL INTERPRETATIONS, Bloom studies the amiable character of Bottom.]

I wish Shakespeare had given us Peter Quince's ballet (ballad), but he may have been too wise to attempt the poem. *A Midsummer Night's Dream*, for me, is Puck and Bottom, and I prefer Bottom. Perhaps we reduce to Puckish individuals or Bottoms. Pucks are more charming, but Bottoms are rather more amiable. Shakespeare's Bottom is surpassingly amiable, and I agree with Northrop Frye that Bottom is the only mortal with experience of the visionary center of the play. As the possible lover (however briefly) of the Fairy Queen, Bottom remains a lasting reproach to our contemporary fashion of importing sacred violence, bestiality, and all manner of sexual antics into Shakespeare's most fragile of visionary dramas. For who could be more mild mannered, better natured, or sweetly humorous than the unfailingly gentle Bottom? Titania ends up despising him, but he is simply too good for her!

Bottom, when we first encounter him, is already a Malaprop, inaccurate at the circumference, as it were, but sound at the core, which is what his name means, the center of the skein upon which a weaver's wool is wound. And surely that is his function in the play; he is its core, and also he is the most original figure in *A Midsummer Night's Dream*. Self-assertive, silly, ignorant, he remains a personage of absolute good will, a kind of remote ancestor to Joyce's amiable Poldy. Transformed into an outward monstrosity by Puck, he yet retains his courage, kindness, and humor, and goes through his uncanny experience totally unchanged within. His initial dialogue with Titania is deliciously ironic, and he himself is in full control of the irony. ⟨ . . . ⟩

> TATANIA: I pary thee, gentle mortal, sing again.
> Mine ear is much enamored of thy note;
> So is mine eye enthralled to thy shape;
> And thy fair virtue's force (perforce) doth move me
> On the first view to say, to swear, I love thee.
> BOTTOM: Methinks, mistress, you should have little reason
> for that. And yet, to say the truth, reason and love keep
> little company together now-a-days, The more the pity
> that some honest neighbors will not make them friends.
> Nay, I can gleek upon occasion.
> TITANIA: Thou art as wise as thou art beautiful.
> BOTTOM: Not so, neither; but if I had wit enough to get out of this
> wood, I have enough to serve mine own turn.

Knowing that he lacks both beauty and wisdom, Bottom is realistic enough to see that the faery queen is beautiful but not wise. Charmed by (and charming to) the elve foursome of Peaseblossom, Cobweb, Moth, and Mustardseed, Bottom makes us aware that they mean no more and no less to him than Titania does. Whether or not he has made love to Titania, a subject of some nasty debate among our critical contemporaries, seems to me quite irrelevant. ⟨ . . . ⟩

What does matter is that he is sublimely unchanged, for worse or for better, when he wakes up from his bottomless dream:

> BOTTOM: [*Awaking.*] When my cue comes, call me, and I will answer. My next is, "Most fair Pyramus." Heigh-ho! Peter Quince! Flute the bellowsmender! Snout the tinker! Starveling! God's my life, stol'n hence, and left me asleep! I have had a most rare vision. I have had a dream, past the wit of man to say what dream it was. Man is but an ass, if he go about [t'] expound this dream. Methought I was—there is no man can tell what. Me thought I was, and methought I had—but man is but [a patch'd] fool, if he will offer to say what methought I had. The eye of man hath not heard, the ear of man hath not seen, man's hand is not able to taste, his tongue to conceive, nor his heart to report, what my dream was. I will get Peter Quince to write a ballet of this dream. It shall be call'd "Bottom's Dream," because it hath no bottom; and I will sing it in the latter end of a play, before the Duke. Peradventure, to make it the more gracious, I shall sing it at her death.

Bottom's revision of 1 Corinthians 2:9–10 is the heart of the matter:

> Eye hath not seen, nor ear heard, neither have entered into the heart of man, the things which God hath prepared for them that love him. But God hath revealed them unto us by his Spirit.
>
> (St. Paul)

> The eye of man hath not heard, the ear of man hath not seen, man's hand is not able to taste, his tongue to conceive, not his heart to report, what my dream was.
>
> (Bottom)

Bottom's scrambling of the senses refuses St. Paul's easy supernaturalism, with its dualistic split between flesh and spirit. Our prophet Bottom is a monist, and so his dream urges upon us a synesthetic reality, fusing flesh and spirit. That Bottom is one for whom God has prepared the things revealed by his Spirit is made wonderfully clear in the closing dialogue between the benign weaver and Theseus:

BOTTOM: [*Starting up.*] No, I assure you, the wall is down that parted their fathers. Will it please you to see the epilogue, or to hear a Bergomask dance between two of our company?
THESEUS: No epilogue, I pray you; for your play needs no excuse.

Only Bottom could assure us that the wall is down that parted all our fathers. The weaver's common sense and natural goodness bestow upon him an aesthetic dignity, homely and humane, that is the necessary counterpoise to the world of Puck that otherwise would ravish reality away in Shakespeare's visionary drama.

—Harold Bloom, Introduction to *William Shakespeare's A Midsummer Night's Dream*, ed. Harold Bloom (New York: Chelsea House Publishers, 1987): pp. 1–3.

Plot Summary of
The Merchant of Venice

The Merchant of Venice must have been written in August 1596. Because of the strong verbal parallels, scholars generally agree that Shakespeare's *Merchant* is indebted to Marlowe's *The Jew of Malta*, first performed in 1589. One of Shakespeare's story lines—the bond plot—is of ancient origin and was very popular in tales from Persia and India. Shakespeare's immediate source was Ser Giovanni's *Il Pecarone*, written at the end of the fourteenth century and printed in Italian in 1558. (Shakespeare may have been able to read it in its original Italian.) Also, critics debate that a lost play entitled *The Jew* could have been one of his direct sources. The second story—the casket plot—had had a long tradition even before Boccaccio and Gover exploited it in the fourteenth century. It has been suggested that *The Merchant of Venice* has all the elements of tragedy apart from its comic solution. One thing is clear, however: the characters, with their indisputable reality, can be subject to many different interpretations.

Act I, scene one opens with Antonio's words about his sadness. Antonio is a Venetian merchant, who invests his wealth in trade ships. His friend, Bassanio, wants to marry Portia of Belmont, and he feels he can win her only if he has enough money (his own he has already carelessly spent), and he asks Antonio for a loan of 3000 ducats. Antonio readily accedes although he doesn't have the funds at hand, but he promises he will try to borrow money for him in Venice.

In scene two Shakespeare introduces the casket plot. We find Portia talking to her waiting-maid, Nerissa, about the strange conditions of her father's will. According to it, Portia may marry only the man who chooses the right casket among three which are made of gold, silver, and lead. Portia has met a few suitors but likes none of them. At the end of this scene a messenger enters to announce the Prince of Morocco.

Scene three finds Bassanio in Venice, in the middle of a conversation with Shylock, a wealthy Jew, a usurer. On Antonio's behalf, Bassanio asks for a loan of 3000 ducats for three months. Antonio enters and, from the conversation between Shylock and Antonio, it is more than obvious that they are not fond of each other. Shylock agrees to lend the money under the condition that Antonio sign a bond stipulating that he will give a pound of his own flesh if he cannot repay the debt on time. Bassanio protests, but Antonio is confident that his ships will come back even earlier than the set date.

Act II, scene one shows the Prince of Morocco, Portia's suitor, who accepts the terms of the will: If he chooses the wrong casket, he may never seek to get married.

In scene two Launcelot Gobbo, a clown, servant to Shylock, wonders if he should try to find a new master. Launcelot's father asks Bassanio to take his son into service and Bassanio accepts. Bassanio's talkative friend, Gratiano, accompanies Bassanio to Belmont as well.

In scene three Jessica, Shylock's daughter, is introduced. She gives a letter to Launcelot to deliver to Lorenzo, Bassiano's more dreamy than practical friend. Through a six-line soliloquy, Jessica reveals her shame that she is her father's daughter as well as her wish to marry Lorenzo and become a Christian wife.

In scene four, four friends (Lorenzo, Gratiano, Solanio, and Salerio) are trying to put on a masque for Bassanio but are not satisfied with the preparations. Lorenzo reads Jessica's letter (in which she instructs him to rescue her), and he asks his friends for help.

In scene five Bassanio invites Shylock to dinner, which he grudgingly accepts. He commands Jessica to take care of the house. Launcelot manages to tell Jessica that Lorenzo will come for her later that night.

Scene six presents Gratiano and Salerio waiting for Lorenzo in front of Shylock's house. Lorenzo arrives, and Jessica throws him a casket containing her father's fortune. Disguised as a boy, she elopes with Lorenzo. Antonio enters to announce that there will not be any masque: the wind has changed and Bassanio is now ready to sail to Belmont.

In scene seven the Prince of Morocco chooses the gold casket, only to find in it a skull and the warning never to make a choice according to appearances.

In scene eight Salerio and Solanio chatter about Shylock's misfortune (he lost his daughter and his fortune). Salerio also mentions that he heard about the wreckage of an Italian ship in the English

Channel; he also worries about telling this news to Antonio, who is already saddened by Bassanio's departure.

In scene nine the Prince of Arragon tries to win Portia. He picks the silver casket only to find in it the picture of a "blinking idiot." After he is dismissed, a messenger announces another suitor. Nerissa prays: "Bassanio, Lord Love, if thy will it be" (II, ix, 109).

Act III, scene one begins with the news (that Salario discloses) that it was Antonio's ship which sank in the English Channel. Shylock enters, furious at his daughter's flight. Tubal, Shylock's friend, reports that Jessica and Lorenzo are lavishly spending money in Genoa and that Antonio is "certainly undone." Shylock urges Tubal to go to the synagogue in order to commence a lawsuit against Antonio.

Scene two is full of dramatic and emotional tension. Portia asks Bassanio to pause a day or two before he chooses the casket. Bassanio refuses and he picks the lead casket with "fair Portia's counterfeit" in it. He claims his bride, and Portia, overjoyed, gives him a ring, which, she insists "when you part from, lose, or give away,/Let it presage the ruin of your love,/And be my vantage to exclaim on you" (III, ii, 176–78). Gratiano is successful in courting Nerissa and announces that they will marry. To complete the trio of lovers, Lorenzo and Jessica arrive. However, Bassanio's joy is soon blighted. They also bring the news that Antonio is ruined because all his ships failed to return, and his bond to Shylock forfeited. When Portia hears of the loan of 3000 ducats, she offers to pay back double and dispatches Bassanio to Venice at once.

In scene three Antonio makes a last effort to have Shylock listen to him, but at Antonio's every request, he answers with "I'll have my bond." The scene closes with Antonio's prayer for Bassanio to come and see him before he dies.

In scene four Portia declares to Lorenzo and Jessica that she and Nerissa are going to a nunnery where they will stay until Bassanio and Gratiano come back. Instead of doing that, Portia sends her messenger, Balthazar, to her cousin, Dr. Bellario of Paduo. Her plan is to go, disguised as a man, to Venice and save Antonio.

In scene five the clown, Launcelet Gobbo, makes fun of Jessica and Lorenzo.

Act IV, scene one opens at the court of Venice, just as Antonio's trial begins. Shylock doesn't give up on his demand that the terms of his bond be fulfilled. "You'll ask me why I rather choose to have/A weight of carrion flesh than to receive/Three thousand ducats. I'll not answer that,/But say it is my humour. Is it answered?" (IV, i, 41–3). Bassanio calls him an "unfeeling man." At that point, Portia enters, disguised as a lawyer supposedly sent from Dr. Bellario. She acts as the "most righteous judge," and, in her first attempts, tries to soften Shylock's heart—but in vain. Finally, after carefully examining the contract, she awards the pound of flesh, only under the condition that if one drop of Christian blood is shed, all his lands and goods will be confiscated. Shylock, realizing that he is defeated, asks to accept the offer of 6000 ducats, only to hear that once he refused it in the court, he can no longer claim it. Portia now finds Shylock, an alien, guilty of threatening the life of a Venetian citizen. As a penalty, he has to give half of his fortune to Antonio, and half to the state. Antonio refuses the deal; instead he demands that, first, Shylock become a Christian and second, that after his death all of his possessions go to his daughter and Lorenzo. Shylock, a broken man, has no other choice than to do what he is asked. Portia, disguised, refuses Bassanio's award of 3000 ducats and, testing him, she asks for nothing else but the ring she herself has given him. At first, Bassanio refuses, but persuaded by Antonio, sends Gratiano after Portia with the ring.

In scene two Gratiano gives the ring to Portia, and Nerissa wants to see if she can obtain the ring from her husband, Gratiano.

In the final scene (Act V, scene one) Portia and Nerissa return to Belmont just in time for Bassanio's and Gratiano's arrival with Antonio. They each demand their rings and accuse their husbands of unfaithfulness. As a surprise to all, they reveal that Portia was the lawyer who saved Antonio. Word also comes that a few of Antonio's ships have returned home. The play turns out to be tragedy only for Shylock. ❁

List of Characters in
The Merchant of Venice

Antonio is the merchant of Venice, a wealthy gentleman of rather melancholy disposition. He borrows money from Shylock in order to help his friend Bassanio, and signs a bond agreeing to forfeit a pound of flesh if he doesn't pay the debt on time. He is saved from that fate by Portia.

Shylock is a rich Jew, cruelly treated by Antonio. He lends Bassanio 3000 ducats on condition that unless paid on time, he will cut a pound of flesh from the body of Antonio. He is defeated by Portia in court, and, unconvincingly enough, when demanded to be converted to a Christian, he replies "I am content." His daughter, Jessica, escapes from him with his fortune, and Shylock ends the play as a broken man.

Bassanio is Antonio's friend, presented as an irresponsible, clever young man. He wants to court Portia (partly for her wealth) and asks for money from Antonio. Bassanio chooses the right casket and marries Portia.

Portia, of Belmont, is a "lady richly left." She marries Bassanio. It is she who, disguised as a doctor of law, successfully defends Antonio and brings about Shylock's ruin. She is noted for her speech on mercy in Act IV, scene one.

Nerissa is Portia's waiting maid who marries Gratiano. When Portia disguises herself as a doctor of law, Nerissa acts as a clerk.

Gratiano is one of Bassanio's friends. He is presented as a talkative and witty character, "too wild, too rude, and bold of voice." He marries Nerissa.

Lorenzo is a friend of Bassanio, who elopes with Jessica, Shylock's daughter.

Jessica is Shylock's daughter. She runs away with Lorenzo and takes her father's fortune.

Launcelot Gobbo is a servant first of Shylock and, after leaving him, of Bassanio. He helps Jessica escape with Lorenzo.

The Duke of Venice presides at the trial of Shylock against Antonio.

Salanio, Salarino, and **Salerio** are friends of Antonio and Bassanio. ❈

Critical Views on
The Merchant of Venice

August Wilhelm Schlegel on Shakespeare's Characterization

[August Wilhelm Schlegel (1767–1845) was a German scholar and critic, and one of the most influential advocates of the German Romantic movement. He was also an Orientalist and a poet. His greatest achievement is his translation of Shakespeare. In his famous book *Lectures on Dramatic Art and Literature* (1809–1811), excerpted here, Schlegel praises Shylock as a masterpiece of characterization.]

The *Merchant of Venice* is one of Shakespeare's most perfect works: popular to an extraordinary degree, and calculated to produce the most powerful effect on the stage, and at the same time a wonder of ingenuity and art for the reflecting critic. Shylock, the Jew, is one of the inimitable masterpieces of characterization which are to be found only in Shakespeare. It is easy for both poet and player to exhibit a caricature of national sentiments, modes of speaking, and gestures. Shylock, however, is everything but a common Jew: he possesses a strongly-marked and original individuality, and yet we perceive a light touch of Judaism in everything he says or does. We almost fancy we can hear a light whisper of the Jewish accent even in the written words, such as we sometimes still find in the higher classes, notwithstanding their social refinement. In tranquil moments, all that is foreign to the European blood and Christian sentiments is less perceptible, but in passion the national stamp comes out more strongly marked. All these inimitable niceties the finished art of a great actor can alone properly express. Shylock is a man of information, in his own way, even a thinker, only he has not discovered the region where human feelings dwell; his morality is founded on the disbelief in goodness and magnanimity. The desire to avenge the wrongs and indignities heaped upon his nation is, after avarice, his strongest spring of action. His hate is naturally directed chiefly against those Christians who are actuated by truly Christian sentiments: a disinterested love of our neighbour seems to him the most unrelenting persecution of the Jews. The letter of the law is his idol; he refuses to lend an ear to the voice of mercy, which, from the mouth of Portia, speaks to him with heavenly eloquence: he insists on rigid and inflexible justice, and at last it recoils on his own head. Thus he becomes a symbol of the general history of his unfortunate nation. The melancholy and self-sacrificing magnanimity of Antonio is affectingly sublime. Like a princely merchant, he is surrounded with a whole train of noble friends. The contrast which this forms to the selfish cruelty of the usurer Shylock was necessary to redeem the honour of human nature. The danger which almost to the close of the fourth act, hangs over Antonio, and which the imagination is almost afraid to approach, would fill the mind with too painful anxiety, if the poet did not also provide for its recreation and diversion. This is effected in an especial manner by the scenes at Portia's country-seat, which transport the spectator into quite another world. And yet they are closely connected with the main business by the chain of cause and effect: Bassanio's preparations for his courtship are the cause of Antonio's subscribing the dangerous bond; and Portia again by the counsel and advice of her uncle, a famous lawyer, effects the safety of her lover's friend. But the relations of the dramatic composition are the while admirably observed in yet another respect. The trial between Shylock and Antonio is indeed recorded as being a real event, still, for all that, it must ever remain an unheard-of and singular case. Shakespeare has therefore associated it with a love intrigue not less extraordinary: the one consequently is rendered natural and probable by means of the other. A rich, beautiful and clever heiress, who can only be won by the solving of a riddle—the locked caskets— the foreign princes, who come to try the venture—all this powerfully excites the imagination with the splendour of an olden tale of marvels. The two scenes in which, first the Prince of Morocco, in the language of Eastern hyperbole, and then the self-conceited Prince of Arragon, make their choice among the caskets, serve merely to raise our curiosity, and give employment to our wits; but on the third, where the two lovers stand trembling before the inevitable choice, which in one moment must unite or separate them forever, Shakespeare has lavished all the charms of feeling—all the magic of poesy. We share in the rapture of Portia and Bassanio at the fortunate choice: we easily conceive why they are so fond of each other, for they are both most deserving of love. The judgement scene, with which the fourth act is occupied, is in itself a perfect drama, concentrating in itself the interest of the whole. The knot is now untied, and according to the common ideas of theatrical satisfaction, the curtain ought to drop.

But the poet was unwilling to dismiss his audience with the gloomy impressions which Antonio's expectation, and the condemnation of Shylock, were calculated to leave behind them; he has therefore added the fifth act by way of a musical afterlude in the piece itself. The episode of Jessica, the fugitive daughter of the Jew, in whom Shakespeare has contrived to throw a veil of sweetness over the national features, and the artifice by which Portia and her companion are enabled to rally their newly-married husbands, supply him with the necessary materials. The scene opens with the playful prattling of two lovers in a summer evening; it is followed by soft music, and a rapturous eulogy on this powerful disposer of the human mind and the world; the principal characters then make their appearance, and after a simulated quarrel, which is gracefully maintained, the whole end with the most exhilarating mirth.

—August Wilhelm Schlegel, *Lectures on Dramatic Art and Literature* (London: George Bell & Sons, 1886): 388–390.

WILLIAM HAZLITT ON THE MASTERPIECE OF SHYLOCK

[William Hazlitt (1778–1830) is a British writer best remembered for his essays, which are read for sheer enjoyment of his brilliant intellect and for permanent value for their humanity. Among his many works are *Lectures on the English Poets* (1818), *Lectures on the English Comic Writers* (1819), and *Liber Amoris,* in which he describes the suffering of his love affair that ended disastrously. In this extract taken from his *Characters of Shakespear's Plays* (1817), Hazlitt studies Shylock and the trial scene, which he considers "a master-piece of dramatic skill."]

Shylock is *a good hater;* "a man no less sinned against than sinning." If he carries his revenge too far, yet he has strong grounds for "the lodged hate he bears Antonio," which he explains with equal force of eloquence and reason. He seems the depositary of the vengeance of his race; and though the long habit of brooding over daily insults and injuries has crusted over his temper with inveterate misanthropy, and hardened him against the contempt of mankind, this adds but little to the triumphant pretensions of his enemies. There is a strong, quick, and deep sense of justice mixed up with the gall and bitterness of his resentment. The constant apprehension of being burnt alive, plundered, banished, reviled, and trampled on, might be supposed to sour the most forbearing nature, and to take something from that "milk of human kindness," with which his persecutors contemplated his indignities. The desire of revenge is almost inseparable from the sense of wrong; and we can hardly help sympathising with the proud spirit, hid beneath his "Jewish gabardine," stung to madness by repeated undeserved provocations, and labouring to throw off the load of obloquy and oppression heaped upon him and all his tribe by one desperate act of "lawful" revenge, till the ferociousness of the means by which he adheres to it, turn us against him; but even at last, when disappointed of the sanguinary revenge with which he had glutted his hopes, and exposed to beggary and contempt by the letter of the law on which he had insisted with so little remorse, we pity him, and think him hardly dealt with by his judges. In all his answers and retorts upon his adversaries, he has the best not only of the argument but of the question, reasoning on their own principles and practice. ⟨ . . . ⟩

The whole of the trial-scene, both before and after the entrance of Portia, is a master-piece of dramatic skill. The legal acuteness, the passionate declamations, the sound maxims of jurisprudence, the wit and irony interspersed in it, the fluctuations of hope and fear in the different persons, and the completeness and suddenness of the catastrophe, cannot be surpassed. Shylock, who is his own counsel, defends himself well, and is triumphant on all the general topics that are urged against him, and only fails through a legal flaw. Take the following as an instance:—

> "SHYLOCK: What judgement shall I dread, doing no wrong?
> You have among you many a purchas'd slave,
> Which like your asses, and your dogs, and mules,
> You use in abject and in slavish part,
> Because you bought them:—shall I say to you,
> Let them be free, marry them to your heirs?
> Why sweat they under burdens? let their beds
> Be made as soft as yours, and let their palates
> Be season'd with such viands? you will answer,
> The slaves are ours:—so do I answer you:

The pound of flesh, which I demand of him,
Is dearly bought, is mine, and I will have it:
If you deny me, fie upon your law!
There is no force in the decrees of Venice:
I stand for judgment: answer; shall I have it?"

The keenness of his revenge awakes all his faculties; and he beats back all opposition to his purpose, whether grave or gay, whether of wit or argument, with an equal degree of earnestness and self-possession. His character is displayed as distinctly in other less prominent parts of the play, and we may collect from a few sentences the history of his life—his descent and origin, his thrift and domestic economy, his affection for his daughter, whom he loves next to his wealth, his courtship and his first present to Leah, his wife! "I would not have parted with it" (the ring which he first gave her) "for a wilderness of monkeys!" What a fine Hebraism is implied in this expression!

—William Hazlitt, *Characters of Shakespear's Plays: Lectures on the English Poets* (London: Macmillan, 1817, 1925): 166–168.

ELMER EDGAR STOLL ON SHYLOCK'S PENALTY

[Elmer Edgar Stoll was Professor of English at the University of Minnesota. His books include *Shakespeare and Other Masters* and *Art and Artifice in Shakespeare*. This extract is taken from his essay "Shylock" first published in the *Journal of English and Germanic Philology* (1911). Here he holds that Shylock's penalty is the heaviest to be found in all the pound-of-flesh stories.]

Hero or not, Shylock is given a villain's due. His is the heaviest penalty to be found in all the pound of flesh stories, including that in *Il Pecorone*, which served as a model for this. Not in the Servian, the Persian, the African version, or even that of the *Cursor Mundi* does the money-lender suffer like Shylock—impoverishment, sentence of death, and an outrage done to his faith from which Jews were guarded even by decrees of German Emperors and Roman pontiffs. It was in the old play, perhaps, but that Shakespeare retained it shows his indifference to the amenities, to say the least, as regards either Jews or Judaism. Shylock's griefs excite no commiseration; indeed, as they press upon him they are barbed with gibes and jeers. The lot of Coriolanus is not dissimilar, but we know that the poet is with him. We know that the poet is not with Shylock, for on that head, in this play as in every other, the impartial, inscrutable poet leaves little or nothing to suggestion or surmise. As is his custom elsewhere, by the comments of the good characters, by the method pursued in the disposition of scenes, and by the downright avowals of soliloquy, he constantly sets us right. ⟨ . . . ⟩

Only twice does Shakespeare seem to follow Shylock's pleadings and reasonings with any sympathy—"Hath a dog money?" in the first scene in which he appears, and "Hath not a Jew eyes?" in the third act—but a bit too much has been made of this. Either plea ends in such fashion as to alienate the audience. To Shylock's reproaches the admirable Antonio, "one of the gentlest and humblest of all the men in Shakespeare's theatre," praised and honored by every one but Shylock, retorts, secure in his virtue, that he is just as like to spit on him and spurn him again. And Shylock's celebrated justification of his race runs headlong into a justification of his villainy:—"The villainy which you teach me I will execute, and it shall go hard but I will better the instruction." "Hath not a Jew eyes?" and he proceeds to show that your Jew is no less than a man, and as such has a right, not to respect or compassion as the critics of a century have had it, but to revenge. Neither large nor lofty are his claims. Quite as vigorously and, in that day, with as much reason, the detestable and abominable Aaron defends his race and color, and Edmund, the dignity of bastards. The worst of his villains Shakespeare allows to plead their cause: their confidences in soliloquy, if not, as here, slight touches in the plea itself, sufficiently counteract any too favorable impression. This, on the face of it, is a plea for indulging in revenge with all its rigors; not a word is put in for the nobler side of Jewish character; and in lending Shylock his eloquence Shakespeare is but giving the devil his due.

—Elmer Edgar Stoll, "Shylock," *Journal of English and Germanic Philology* 10 (1911). Reprinted in *Major Literary Characters: Shylock*, ed. Harold Bloom (New York: Chelsea House: 1991): pp. 86–89.

[Sigmund Freud (1856–1939) is the founder of psychoanalysis. Among his most important books translated into English are *The Interpretation of Dreams* (1913) and *General Introduction to Psychoanalysis* (1920). Freud frequently devoted his attention to the study of literature from a psychoanalytic aspect. In this extract Freud sees in three caskets symbolic substitutions for women.]

The first of these scenes is the suitors' choice between the three caskets in *The Merchant of Venice*. The fair and wise Portia is bound at her father's bidding to take as her husband only that one of her suitors who chooses the right casket from among the three before him. The three caskets are of gold, silver, and lead: the right casket is the one that contains her portrait. Two suitors have already departed unsuccessful: they have chosen gold and silver. Bassanio, the third, decides in favour of lead; thereby he wins the bride, whose affection was already his before the trial of fortune. Each of the suitors gives reasons for his choice in a speech in which he praises the metal he prefers and depreciates the other two. The most difficult task thus falls to the share of the fortunate third suitor; what he finds to say in glorification of lead as against gold and silver is little and has a forced ring. If in psycho-analytic practice we were confronted with such a speech, we should suspect that there were concealed motives behind the unsatisfying reasons produced.

Shakespeare did not himself invent this oracle of the choice of a casket; he took it from a tale in the *Gesta Romanorum,* in which a girl has to make the same choice to win the Emperor's son. Here too the third metal, lead, is the bringer of fortune. It is not hard to guess that we have here an ancient theme, which requires to be interpreted, accounted for and traced back to its origin. A first conjecture as to the meaning of this choice between gold, silver, and lead is quickly confirmed by a statement of Stucken's, who has made a study of the same material over a wide field. He writes: "The identity of Portia's three suitors is clear from their choice: the Prince of Morocco chooses the gold casket—he is the sun; the Prince of Arragon chooses the silver casket—he is the moon; Bassanio chooses the leaden casket—he is the star youth." In support of this explanation he cites an episode from the Estonian folk-epic "Kalewipoeg," in which the three suitors appear undisguisedly as the sun, moon, and star youths (the last being "the Pole-star's eldest boy") and once again the bride falls to the lot of the third.

Thus our little problem has led us to an astral myth! The only pity is that with this explanation we are not at the end of the matter. The question is not exhausted, for we do not share the belief of some investigators that myths were read in the heavens and brought down from earth; we are more inclined to judge with Otto Rank that they were projected on to the heavens after having arisen elsewhere under purely human conditions. It is in this human content that our interest lies.

Let us look once more at our material. In the Estonian epic, just as in the tale from the *Gesta Romanorum,* the subject is a girl choosing between three suitors; in the scene from *The Merchant of Venice* the subject is apparently the same, but at the same time something appears in it that is in the nature of an inversion of the theme: a *man* chooses between the three—caskets. If what we were concerned with were a dream, it would occur to us at once that caskets are also women, symbols of what is essential in a woman, and therefore of a woman herself—like coffers, boxes, cases, baskets, and so on. If we boldly assume that there are symbolic substitutions of the same kind in myths as well, then the casket scene in *The Merchant of Venice* really becomes the inversion we suspected. With a wave of the wand, as though we were in a fairy tale, we have stripped the astral garment from our theme; and now we see that the theme is a human one, *a man's choice between three women.*

This same content, however, is to be found in another scene of Shakespeare's, in one of his most powerfully moving dramas; not the choice of a bride this time, yet linked by many hidden similarities to the choice of the casket in *The Merchant of Venice.* The old King Lear resolves to divide his kingdom while he is still alive among his three daughters, in proportion to the amount of love that each of them expresses for him. The two elder ones, Goneril and Regan, exhaust themselves in asseverations and laudations of their love for him; the third, Cordelia, refuses to do so. He should have recognized the unassuming, speechless love of his daughter and rewarded it, but he does not recognize it. He disowns Cordelia, and divides the kingdom between the other two, to his own and the general ruin. Is not this once more the scene of a choice between three women, of whom the youngest is the best, the most excellent one?

There will at once occur to us other scenes from myths, fairy tales and literature, with the same situation as their content. The shepherd Paris has to choose between three goddesses, of whom he declares the third to be the most beautiful. Cinderella, again, is the youngest daughter, who is preferred by the prince to her two elder sisters. Psyche, in Apuleius's story, is the youngest and fairest of three sisters. Psyche is, on the one hand, revered as Aphrodite in human form; on the other, she is treated by that goddess as Cinderella was treated by her stepmother and is set the task of sorting a heap of mixed seeds, which she accomplishes with the help of small creatures (doves in the case of Cinderella, ants in the case of Psyche). Anyone who cared to make a wider survey of the material would undoubtedly discover other versions of the same theme preserving the same essential features.

Let us be content with Cordelia, Aphrodite, Cinderella and Psyche. In all the stories the three women, of whom the third is the most excellent one, must surely be regarded as in some way alike if they are represented as sisters. (We must not be led astray by the fact that Lear's choice is between three *daughters;* this may mean nothing more than that he has to be represented as an old man. An old man cannot very well choose between three women in any other way. Thus they become his daughters.)

But who are these three sisters and why must the choice fall on the third? If we could answer this question, we should be in possession of the interpretation we are seeking. We have once already made use of an application of psychoanalytic technique, when we explained the three caskets symbolically as three women. If we have the courage to proceed in the same way, we shall be setting foot on a path which will lead us first to something unexpected and incomprehensible, but which will perhaps, by a devious route, bring us to a goal.

It must strike us that this excellent third woman has in several instances certain peculiar qualities besides her beauty. They are qualities that seem to be tending towards some kind of unity; we must certainly not expect to find them equally well marked in every example. Cordelia makes herself unrecognizable, inconspicuous like lead, she remains dumb, she "loves and is silent." Cinderella hides so that she cannot be found. We may perhaps be allowed to equate concealment and dumbness. These would of course be only two instances out of the five we have picked out. But there is an imitation of the same thing to be found, curiously enough, in two other cases. We have decided to compare Cordelia, with her obstinate refusal, to lead. In Bassanio's short speech while he is choosing the casket, he says of lead (without in any way leading up to the remark):

"Thy paleness moves me more than eloquence."
("Plainness" according to another reading.)

That is to say: "Thy plainness moves me more than the blatant nature of the other two." Gold and silver are "loud"; lead is dumb—in fact like Cordelia, who "loves and is silent."

In the ancient Greek accounts of the Judgement of Paris, nothing is said of any such reticence on the part of Aphrodite. Each of the three goddesses speaks to the youth and tries to win him by promises. But, oddly enough, in a quite modern handling of the same scene this characteristic of the third one which has struck us makes its appearance again. In the libretto of Offenbach's *La Belle Hélène*, Paris, after telling of the solicitations of the other two goddesses, describes Aphrodite's behaviour in this competition for the beauty-prize:

La troisième, ah! la troisième . . .
La troisième ne dit rien.
Elle eut le prix tout de même . . .
(Literally: "The third one, ah! the third one . . . the third one said
nothing. She won the prize all the same."—The quotation is from Act
I, scene 7, of Meilhac and Halévy's libretto. In the German version
used by Freud "the third one" "*blieb stumm*"—"remained dumb.")

If we decide to regard the peculiarities of our "third one" as concentrated in her "dumbness," then psycho-analysis will tell us that in dreams dumbness is a common representation of death.

More than ten years ago a highly intelligent man told me a dream which he wanted to use as evidence of the telepathic nature of dreams. In it he saw an absent friend from whom he had received no news for a very long time, and reproached him energetically for his silence. The friend made no reply. It afterwards turned out that he had met his death by suicide at about the time of the dream. Let us leave the problem of telepathy on one side: there seems, however, not to be any doubt that here the dumbness in the dream represented death. Hiding and being unfindable—a thing which confronts the prince in the fairy tale of Cinderella three times, is another unmistakable symbol of death in dreams; so, too, is a marked pallor, of which the "paleness" of the lead in one reading of Shakespeare's text is a reminder. It would be very much easier for us to transpose these interpretations from the language of dreams to the mode of expression used in the myth that is now under consideration if we could make it seem probable that dumbness must be interpreted as a sign of being dead in productions other than dreams.

At this point I will single out the ninth story in Grimm's *Fairy Tales,* which bears the title "The Twelve Brothers." A king and a queen have twelve children, all boys. The king declares that if the thirteenth child is a girl, the boys will have to die. In expectation of her birth he has twelve coffins made. With their mother's help the twelve sons take refuge in a hidden wood, and swear death to any girl they meet. A girl is born, grows up, and learns one day from her mother that she has had twelve brothers. She decides to seek them out, and in the wood she finds the youngest; he recognizes her, but is anxious to hide her on account of the brothers' oath. The sister says: "I will gladly die, if by so doing I can save my twelve brothers." The brothers welcome her affectionately, however, and she stays with them and looks after their house for them. In a little garden beside the house grow twelve lilies. The girl picks them and gives one to each brother. At that moment the brothers are changed into ravens, and disappear, together with the house and garden. (Ravens are spirit-birds; the killing of the twelve brothers by their sister is represented by the picking of the flowers, just as it is at the beginning of the story by the coffins and the disappearance of the brothers.) The girl, who is once more ready to save her brothers from death, is now told that as a condition she must be dumb for seven years, and not speak a single word. She submits to the test, which brings her herself into mortal danger. She herself, that is, dies for her brothers, as she promised to do before she met them. By remaining dumb she succeeds at last in setting the ravens free.

—Sigmund Freud, "The Theme of the Three Caskets" *The Standard Edition of the Complete Psychological Works of Sigmund Freud,* 12 (New York: The Hogarth Press, (1911–1913, 1958). Reprinted in *Major Literary Characters: Shylock,* ed. Harold Bloom (New York: Chelsea House: 1991): 7–11.

[Graham Bradshaw is a professor in English at the University
of St. Andrews. In this extract, taken from his book *Shakespeare's Scepticism* (1987), Bradshaw examines the play of
irony in the characters.]

For as Jessica rounds up her father's ducats, Leah's turquoise and other
swag—all of which will be exhausted by Act 5, when these lovers prettily
admit to being 'starved' for fresh supplies of 'manna' (5.1.293–4)—her
no less consciously pretty prattling shows that she is entirely preoccu-
pied with her *appearance*. She feels 'shame' and wants to be 'obscur'd'—
because she is in a boy's clothes, *not* because she is stealing:

> Heere, catch this casket, it is worth the paines,
> I am glad 'tis night, you do not looke on me,
> For I am much asham'd of my exchange:
> But love is blinde, and lovers cannot see
> The pretty follies that themselves commit,
> For if they could, *Cupid* himself would blush
> To see me thus transformed to a boy . . .
> What, must I hold a Candle to my shames?
> They in themselves goodsooth are too too light.
> Why 'tis an office of discovery Love,
> And I should be obscur'd . . .
> I will make fast the doores and guild my selfe
> With some more ducats, and be with you straight.
> (2.6.33 f.)

Such prettiness naturally wins the admiration of Gratiano ('Now by
my hood, a gentle, and no Jew') as well as Lorenzo ('true she is, as she
hath prov'd her selfe')—naturally, since Jessica's priorities so clearly
coincide with theirs: fine clothes, affairs, extravagant consumption, a
good time and plenty of money or 'manna', which, like the 'mercie' dispensed in the trial scene, has no heavenly origin.

Here too, the difficulty is that of registering the irony without making it seem heavy-handed or moralistic. It is obvious enough that we
would think very differently of Desdemona if she eloped with bags of
swag, but to make that point of an ironic comedy would be like taking
Egeus' point of view in *A Midsummer Night's Dream*. On the other
hand, we need to see what this comedy is being ironic *about,* and this

scene beautifully shows how Jessica's priorities are, like her 'shames', 'too too light'. *She* does not see that her image of *gilding* might introduce a relevant, Macbeth-like pun on *guilt;* or that it recalls her father's reference to the *varnished* faces of Christian fools, Portia's father's reference to *glistering,* and this play's numerous contrasts (including Lorenzo's admiring reference to the *garnish* of a boy) between more sheen and substance. Her thoughtless reference to love's blindness might prompt *us* to think, once again, of the deception in surfaces, of 'Fancie' and the imagination's shaping fantasies. One effect of these ironies is that *we* cannot be as simply indulgent or simply censorious as these characters are in judging each other; rather, we see how Kingsley Amis's remark on Jane Austen *could* be reapplied to these Venetians, who also indulge where they might censure and censure where they might indulge. The play of irony establishes parallels which the characters never suspect or detect. The high spirits of Portia's 'Let me give light, but let me not be light' (5.1.129), or of her comparison of the candle's light with the shining of 'a good deed in a naughty world' (5.1.90–1), acquire a different resonance if we are thinking of Jessica's 'too too light' or of Portia's 'I can easier teach twentie to follow mine owne teaching'—just as that earlier remark has a different resonance if we are considering its relation to Portia's behaviour in the trial scene, rather than her susceptibility to the gleaming Bassanio.

—Graham Bradshaw, *Shakespeare's Scepticism* (New York: St. Martin's Press, 1987): 30–31.

DEREK COHEN ON SHAKESPEARE'S ANTI-SEMITISM

[Derek Cohen is a professor of English at York University and the author of *Shakespearean Motives* (1988) and *Shakespeare's Culture* (1993). In this extract, Cohen argues that *The Merchant of Venice* is an anti-Semitic play and that the end of the play is "a triumph of ambiguity."]

Current criticism notwithstanding, *The Merchant of Venice* seems to me a profoundly and crudely anti-Semitic play. The debate about its implications has usually been between inexpert Jewish readers and spectators who discern an anti-Semitic core and literary critics (many

of them Jews) who defensively maintain that the Shakespearean sub-
tlety of mind transcends anti-Semitism. The critics' arguments, by
now familiar, center on the subject of Shylock's essential humanity,
point to the imperfections of the Christians, and remind us that
Shakespeare was writing in a period when there were so few Jews in
England that it didn't matter anyway (or, alternatively, that because
there were so few Jews in England Shakespeare had probably never
met one, so he didn't really know what he was doing). Where I believe
the defensive arguments go wrong is in their heavy concentration on
the character of Shylock; they overlook the more encompassing attempt of the play to offer a total poetic image of the Jew. It is all very
well for John Russell Brown to say *The Merchant of Venice* is not anti-
Jewish, and that 'there are only two slurs on Jews in general'; but this
kind of assertion, a common enough one in criticism of the play, cannot account for the fear and shame that Jewish audiences and readers
have always felt from the moment of Shylock's entrance to his final
exit. I wish to argue that these feelings are justified and that such an
intuitive response is more natural than the critical sophistries whose
purpose is to exonerate Shakespeare from the charge of anti-Semitism. Although few writers on the subject are prepared to concede as
much, it is quite possible that Shakespeare didn't give a damn about
Jews or about insulting England's miniscule Jewish community, and
that, if he did finally humanize his Jew, he did so simply to enrich his
drama. It is, of course, interesting to speculate on whether Shakespeare was an anti-Semite, but we cannot rise beyond speculation on
this point.

The image of Jewishness which *The Merchant of Venice* presents is
contrasted with the image of Christianity to which it is made referable
and which ultimately encompasses and overwhelms it. Though it is
simplistic to say that the play equates Jewishness with evil and Christianity with goodness, it is surely reasonable to see a moral relationship between the insistent equation of the *idea* of Jewishness with
acquisitive and material values while the *idea* of Christianity is linked
to the values of mercy and love. In this chapter I wish first of all to
demonstrate that *The Merchant of Venice* is an anti-Semitic play by examining the image of Jewishness which it presents and by placing that
image in the contrasting context of Christianity to which it is auto-
matically made referable. Secondly, I wish to examine the paradox
which follows from my assertion of the anti-Semitic nature of the

play—that is, the way in which Shylock is humanized in his final scene and made simultaneously both the villain of the drama and its unfortunate victim. ⟨ . . . ⟩

I would define an anti-Semitic work of art as one that portrays Jews in a way that makes them objects of antipathy to readers and spectators—objects of scorn, hatred, laughter, or contempt. A careful balance is needed to advance this definition, since it might seem to preclude the possibility of an artist's presenting any Jewish character in negative terms without incurring the charge of anti-Semitism. Obviously, Jews must be allowed to have their faults in art as they do in life. In my view, a work of art becomes anti-Semitic not by virtue of its portrayal of an individual Jew in uncomplimentary terms but solely by its association of negative racial characteristics with the term Jewish or with Jewish characters generally. What we must do, then, is look at the way the word *Jew* is used and how Jews are portrayed in *The Merchant of Venice* as a whole.

The word *Jew* is used 58 times in *The Merchant of Venice*. Variants of the word like *Jewess, Jews, Jew's,* and *Jewish* are used 14 times; *Hebrew* is used twice. There are, then, 74 direct uses of *Jew* and unambiguously related words in the play. Since it will readily be acknowledged that Shakespeare understood the dramatic and rhetorical power of iteration, it must follow that there is a deliberate reason for the frequency of the word in the play. And as in all of Shakespeare's plays, the reason is to surround and inform the repeated term with associations which come more and more easily to mind as it is used. A word apparently used neutrally in the early moments of a play gains significance as it is used over and over; it becomes a term with connotations that infuse it with additional meaning. ⟨ . . . ⟩

And yet, although Shylock is the villain of the play, the critics who have been made uneasy by the characterization of his evil have sensed a dimension of pathos, a quality of humanity, that is part of the play. Audiences and readers have usually found themselves pitying Shylock in the end, even though the play's other characters, having demolished him, hardly give the wicked Jew a second thought. The Christians fail to see the humanity of Shylock, not because they are less sensitive than readers and spectators, but because that humanity emerges only in the end, during the court scene when they are understandably caught up in the atmosphere of happiness that surrounds Antonio's release from death. Audiences and readers, whose attention is likely to be equally shared by Antonio and Shylock, are more aware of what is happening to Shylock. They are therefore aware of the change that is forced upon him. To them he is more than simply an undone villain. He is a suffering human being.

Shylock becomes a pitiable character only during his last appearance in the court of Venice. It is here that he is humanized—during a scene in which he is usually silent. Ironically, it is not in his pleadings or self-justifications that Shylock becomes a sympathetic figure, but in his still and silent transformation from a crowing blood-hungry monster into a quiescent victim whose fate lies in the hands of those he had attempted to destroy. How this transmogrification is accomplished is, perhaps, best explained by Gordon Craig's exquisitely simple observation about the chief character of *The Bells*. Craig remarked that 'no matter who the human being may be, and what his crime, the sorrow which he suffers must appeal to out hearts . . . ' This observation helps explain why the scene of the reversal which turns aside the impending catastrophe of *The Merchant of Venice* does not leave the audience with feelings of mixed delight in the way that the reversals of the more conventional comedies do. The reversal of *The Merchant of Venice* defies a basic premise of the normal moral logic of drama. Instead of merely enjoying the overthrow of an unmitigated villain, we find ourselves pitying him. The conclusion of the play is thus a triumph of ambiguity: Shakespeare has sustained the moral argument which dictates Shylock's undoing while simultaneously compelling us to react on an emotional level more compassionate than intellectual.

—Derek Cohen, *Shakespearean Motives* (London: Macmillan, 1988). Reprinted in *Major Literary Characters: Shylock,* ed. Harold Bloom (New York: Chelsea House: 1991): 305–306, 311–312.

Harold Bloom on Shylock's Forced Conversion

[Harold Bloom is Sterling Professor of the Humanities at Yale University and Berg Professor of English at New York University. He is the author of more than twenty books, including *Shakespeare, the Invention of the Human* (1998), and is the editor of over 40 anthologies and works of literary criticism.

This extract is taken from his Introduction to *William Shake-speare's The Merchant of Venice* in the Chelsea House series MODERN CRITICAL INTERPRETATIONS. Here, Bloom discusses whether Shylock's dramatic consistency is destroyed after his forced conversion.]

Of Shakespeare's displaced spirits, those enigmatic figures who some-times seem to have wandered into the wrong play, Shylock clearly re-mains the most problematical. We need always to keep reminding ourselves that he is a *comic* villain, partly derived from the grandest of Marlovian scoundrels, Barabas, Jew of Malta. In some sense, that should place Shylock in the Machiavellian company of two villains of tragedy, Edmund and Iago, yet none of us wishes to see Shylock there. Edmund and Iago are apocalyptic humorists; self-purged of pathos, they frighten us because continually they invent themselves while ma-nipulating others. Shylock's pathos is weirdly heroic; he was meant to frighten us, to be seen as a nightmare made into flesh and blood, while seeking the audience's flesh and blood. ⟨ . . . ⟩

Of all the enigmas presented by *The Merchant of Venice*, to me the most baffling is Shylock's broken acceptance of forced conversion. Is it persuasive? Surely not, since Shakespeare's Shylock, proud and fierce Jew, scarcely would have preferred Christianity to death. Consistency of character in Shylock admittedly might have cost Shakespeare the comedy of his comedy; a Shylock put to death might have shadowed the ecstasy of Belmont in Act V. But so does the forced conversion, for us, though clearly not for Shakespeare and his contemporary audi-ence. The difficult but crucial question becomes: why did Shakespeare inflict the cruelty of the false conversion, knowing he could not allow Shylock the tragic dignity of dying for his people's faith?

I find it astonishing that this question never has been asked any-where in the published criticism of *The Merchant of Venice*. No other Shakespearean character who has anything like Shylock's representa-tional force is handled so strangely by Shakespeare, and ultimately so inadequately. That Shylock should agree to become a Christian is more absurd than would be the conversion of Coriolanus to the pop-ular party, or Cleopatra's consent to become a vestal virgin at Rome. We sooner could see Falstaff as a monk, than we can contemplate Shylock as a Christian. Shakespeare notoriously possessed the powers both of preternatural irony, and of imbuing a character with more vitality than a play's context could sustain. I cannot better the judgement upon Christian conversion that Launcelot Gobbo makes in his dialogue with the charmingly insufferable Jessica, that Jewish Venetian princess:

> JESSICA: I shall be sav'd by my husband, he hath made me a Christian!
> LAUNCELOT: Truly, the more to blame he; we were Christians enow before, e'en as many as could well live one by another. This making of Christians will raise the price of hogs. If we grow all to be pork-eaters, we shall not shortly have a rasher on the coals for money.

But Shakespeare takes care to distance this irony from the play's comic catastrophe, when the Jew is undone by Christian mercy. It is Antonio, the pious Jew-baiter, who adds to the Duke's pardon the requirement that Shylock immediately become a Christian, after which Shakespeare seems a touch anxious to get Shylock offstage as quietly and quickly as possible:

> DUKE: He shall do this, or else I do recant
> The pardon that I late pronounced here.
> PORTIA: Art thou contented, Jew? what dost thou say?
> SHYLOCK: I am content.
> PORTIA: Clerk begins at 2nd of content. Clerk, draw a deed of gift.
> SHYLOCK: I pray you give me leave to go from hence.
> I am not well. Send the deed after me,
> And I will sign it.

And in a moment, Shylock walks out of the play, to the discord of what must seem to us Gratiano's Nazi-like jeers and threats. In our post-Holocaust universe, how can we accommodate Shylock's "I am content," too broken for irony, too strong for any play whatsoever? That question, I think, is unanswerable, and does not belong to literary criticism anyway. What is essential for criticism is to ask and answer the double question: why did Shakespeare so represent his stage Jew as to make possible the Romantic interpretation that has proceeded from Hazlitt and Henry Irving right through to Harold C. Goddard and innumerable actors in our century, and having done so, why did the playwright then shatter the character's consistency by imposing upon him the acceptance of the humiliating forced conversion to that religion of mercy, the Christianity of Venice? ⟨ . . . ⟩

Indeed, as drama Shylock's "I am content" is necessarily a puzzle, not akin say to Iago's "From this time forth I never will speak word." Iago will die, under torture, in absolute silence: a dramatic death. We anticipate that Shylock the broken new Christian will live in silence:

not a dramatic life. Is it that Shakespeare wished to repeal Shylock, as it were, and so cut away the enormous pathos of the character? We have seen no weaknesses in Shylock's will, no signs indeed that he can serve the function of a comic villain, a new Barabas. No red wig and giant nose will transform the speaker of Shylock's three hundred and sixty dark lines into a two-dimensional character. Shylock, however monstrous his contemplated revenge, is all spirit, malign and concentrated, indifferent to the world and the flesh, unless Antonio be taken to represent both for him. Displaced spirit and so villain as he is, Shylock confronts in the heroically Christian merchant of Venice his tormentor and his double, the play's best Christian, who demonstrates the authenticity of his religious and moral zeal by his prowess in spitting at and cursing Shylock. I intend no irony there, and I fear that I read Shakespeare as he meant to *be* read. And yet every time I teach *The Merchant of Venice,* my students rebel at my insistence that Shylock is not there to be sympathized with, whereas Antonio is to be admired, if we are to read the play that Shakespeare wrote. One had best state this matter very plainly: to recover the comic splendor of *The Merchant of Venice* now, you need to be either a scholar or an anti-Semite, or best of all an anti-Semitic scholar.

—Harold Bloom, Introduction to *William Shakespeare's The Merchant of Venice* (New York: Chelsea House, 1986): pp. 1–3. ❁

Plot Summary of
As You Like It

Shakespeare composed *As You Like It* in 1599, a year before he wrote *Hamlet*. Although the plot is derived almost entirely from Thomas Lodge's pastoral romance *Rosalynde or Euphancus' Golden Legacy*, printed in 1590, there is no equivalent to Shakespeare's characters in Lodge. Although Shakespeare had previously experimented with a reduction of the plot's entanglements, in *As You Like It*, as many critics have observed, almost everything that will happen, happens in the first act. In the rest of the play, cunningly juxtaposed characters, set in the pastoral milieu of the Forest of Arden, ruminate upon contrasting ideas: court or country, nature or fortune, youth or age, active or contemplative life, and, above all, love.

The play opens in the orchard (**Act I,** scene one) with Orlando, the younger brother of Oliver and son of Sir Rowland de Boys, complaining to his servant Adam, that he is kept "rustically at home," away from school, although his father charged his brother Oliver to provide him with a good education. Oliver enters, and Orlando, still angry, seizes him by the throat, asking him either to be allowed to go to school or to be given what has been allotted to him by his father's testament.

Orlando and Adam leave, and Charles, the Duke's wrestler, brings word from the new court. The Duke Senior, the lawful ruler of a French province, has been banished by his younger brother Frederick. He fled, along with a few faithful lords, to the Forest of Arden, a world set apart from the ordinary world. Rosalind, the Duke Senior's daughter, is allowed to stay at court because Celia, the daughter of the usurping Duke, loves her so much that she would either follow her into exile or die without her. Oliver admits to Charles that he would like him to break Orlando's neck in the upcoming wrestling match.

Celia, Rosalind, and Touchstone are introduced in scene two. Celia asks Rosalind to be merry despite the fact that her father is banished. Rosalind suggests that they fall in love for sport, as she does, the moment she lays eyes on Orlando at the wrestling match. The focus of the play's plot is primarily on Orlando and Rosalind's match despite three other parallel affairs that occur: Silvius and Phebe, Touchstone and Audrey, and Oliver and Celia. Rosalind tries to dissuade Orlando from the unequal contest, but he is determined to fight. When he completely overthrows his enemy Charles, Rosalind gives him a chain from her neck. Le Beau advises Orlando to leave the place at once because the Duke is in an ill humor.

In scene three the Duke Frederick's motive for his banishment of Rosalind, is given as simply as it could possibly be: "Grounded upon no other argument/But that the people praise her for her virtues" (I, ii, 269–70). Act I ends with Rosalind disguised as a boy setting out for the Forest of Arden, followed by Celia and the jester Touchstone.

The opening lines of **Act II,** scene one include the Duke Senior's description of life in the Forest of Arden, which strongly contrasts with Frederick's nervous court.

In scene two Frederick loses control when he finds out that his daughter has left with Rosalind. Having discovered from the gentlewoman that Orlando must have been in their company as well, he asks, in almost incoherent sentences, for Oliver. The scene is preparation for Oliver's later banishment.

Orlando finds it necessary to leave because of his brother Oliver's intended mistreatment, as scene three shows. His old servant, Adam, accompanies him and they set out for the Forest of Arden.

Scene four introduces Silvius, the shepherd, who is in love with Phebe, a shepherdess. Rosalind dressed in man's clothes as Ganymede, and Celia, as Aliena, are living as shepherdesses in the Forest of Arden. In the disguise of a man, Rosalind is given double identity: she is a lover, but she can also spoof love.

Scene five opens with a pleasant view of forest life, showing the Duke Senior's Lords dressed as foresters. Amiable Amiens sings the well-known "Under the Greenwood tree" and "Blow, blow, thou winter wind." He is contrasted with cynical Jaques, who throughout this cheerful act speaks in prose while everyone else sings and talks in verse.

In scene six Orlando and Adam become weary and hungry; Orlando wanders into the part of the forest where the Duke Senior and his banished courtiers are (scene seven). Hungry, Orlando attacks the Duke with a drawn sword and demands food. The Duke gently welcomes him to their table, and Orlando feels ashamed of his rude manner. He will not touch a bit until Adam is fed as well. Jaques, in his much-discussed speech, compares the world with a stage and develops a view of humanity by dividing human life into seven stages. In the same scene Jaques talks about old age as a "second childishness," "sans teeth, sans eyes, sans taste, sans everything" (II, vii, 165–6), and as soon as that is spoken, Orlando enters with the old Adam, who embodies the sheer image of loyalty and honesty. Since the Duke Senior finds out that Orlando is the son of his friend, Sir Rowland de Boys, he takes Adam and Orlando under his protection.

As a contrast to newly founded friendship, **Act III,** scene one presents the confrontation at court between the two evil-doers of the play, Duke Frederick and Oliver. Duke Frederick demands that Oliver find his brother Orlando, dead or living, within a year, or he should not come back at all.

Scene two, twice as long as any other in the play, is especially concerned with the game of love. Orlando hangs his verses in praise of Rosalind on trees. When he exits, Touchstone and the shepherd Corin discuss how inadequate the manners of the court are when applied to country life. Rosalind, as Ganymede, reads the verses while Touchstone ridicules them. Celia, after delaying, tells Rosalind that Orlando has written the rhymes. Rosalind tricks Orlando by pretending she is a shepherd, a native of the Forest of Arden, and the scene ends with her promise to cure him of love if only he comes every day to her cot and calls her Rosalind.

Scene three opens with Touchstone's willful display of his love for Audrey, a simple-minded girl; he has also arranged with the vicar of the next village, Sir Oliver Martext, to meet them in the forest and marry them.

Scene four begins in prose and changes to verse after the first 42 lines. Rosalind provokes Celia to talk only of Orlando.

Scene five begins with the entry of Silvius and Phebe and brings shift of tone. The moment Phebe spots the disguised Rosalind she falls in love with her. As the scene ends Phebe leaves with Silvius.

In **Act IV,** scene one the love game reaches its height. Orlando joins Rosalind an hour late, and she gives him her first lesson of love, which is that he should never break a promise in love. Rosalind also merrily cautions him that love is not the tragic matter and people do not die for love ("Men have died from time to time, and worms have eaten them, but not for love" [IV, i, 101–2]). Orlando has to leave to join the Duke Senior but promises he will be back in two hours.

Scene two shows Jaques with some other banished courtiers who have killed a deer. They sing a song celebrating their successful hunt, and they wish to present the deer to the Duke. Johnson called this scene the "noisy scene." The main purpose of it is to fill out the time before Orlando returns.

In scene three Orlando is late for his meeting with Ganymede (as Rosalind). Silvius delivers Phebe's love letter to Rosalind; while reading it aloud Rosalind scolds Silvius. Oliver enters with the report that Orlando has been wounded trying to save him from a lion. The dramatic climax of the scene is when Rosalind, having heard it, faints, just to recover instantly and pretend that she faked the whole act. Oliver doesn't believe her and takes her fainting as a testimony that her passion is earnest.

Act V, scene one presents the conflict between the fourth pair of lovers in the play, Audrey and Touchstone. Audrey objects that Touchstone didn't take advantage of the opportunity to have Sir Oliver Martext marry them. Audrey's former suitor, William, enters, but Touchstone, after showing off his wit, asks him to leave, threatening to kill him ("I will kill thee a hundred and fifty ways") if he still tries to pursue Audrey, who is now his (Touchstone's) property.

Scene two shows a completely reformed Oliver, who has fallen in love with Celia at first sight, and plans to marry her tomorrow and live in the Forest of Arden. Oliver also gives his whole property to Orlando. Orlando is dispirited when he sees happiness in another man's eye because he himself cannot have Rosalind. Ganymede (Rosalind) asks him to be ready tomorrow to get married, to Rosalind if he wills it. She also promises Silvius and Phebe that she will help to make them happy tomorrow.

Touchstone and Audrey anticipate a joyful day in scene three. Two pages appear and sing a song about the pleasures of pastoral love.

The four couples meet at the designated time in the final scene (scene four). Rosalind, still disguised as Ganymede, ties up the ends of the plot by telling Orlando that Rosalind will show up if he wishes to marry her and by demanding a promise from Phebe that she will marry Silvius. Touchstone amuses the whole gathering of the main characters while they wait for Rosalind to appear. Finally, Hyman, the god of marriage, brings in Rosalind and Celia dressed as brides-to-be. Jaques de Boys, the second son of Sir Rowland de Boys, enters and announces that Duke Frederick has become a pious man, after contact with an old religious man, and has bequeathed his crown to his banished brother, Duke Senior. He also has restored all the lands to those who were in exile.

The play ends with Rosalind's epilogue, her last touch to *her* play. ❁

List of Characters in
As You Like It

Duke Senior is the father of Rosalind, who is driven into exile by his brother, Frederick. He lives in the Forest of Arden with his devoted lords. He finds "good in everything." Eventually, at the end of the play, he is restored to his position when Frederick converts to a holy life.

Duke Frederick is the usurping brother who exiles Duke Senior; he also banishes Rosalind for no other reason than "that the people praise her for her virtues." He is the father of Celia. At the end of the play he withdraws from the ceremonious life of the court and devotes himself to religious life.

Amiens is the lord who attends the Duke Senior. His cheerful disposition is in contrast to the cynicism of another lord, Jaques. Amiens is the one who sings two famous songs: "Under the Greenwood Tree" and "Blow, blow, thou winter wind."

Jaques (two characters are named Jaques in this play) is the lord usually spoken of as "the melancholy Jaques," who attends the Duke Senior. He stays in the Forest of Arden although the Duke urges him to return with him to the court. He is presented as one who indulges in pessimism and unsociability. For him, nothing is worth the effort, since life finishes in the grave, anyway.

Charles is the wrestler whom Duke Frederick hires and whom Orlando defeats in the wrestling match.

Oliver is the son of Sir Rowland de Boys, the elder brother of Orlando. He asks Charles to break Orlando's neck. Why? "For my soul, yet I know not why, hates nothing more than he." When he goes to the Forest of Arden on Duke Frederick's demand, Orlando saves his life from the lion, and he atones and marries Celia.

The second character named **Jaques** is the second son of Sir Rowland de Boys. He has a very small role in the final scene of the play: he brings the news of Duke Frederick's conversion and his bequeathal of the crown to his brother, the Duke Senior.

Orlando is presented as the vigorous and sensible youngest son of Sir Rowland de Boys who is mistreated by his brother Oliver. He overthrows Charles, the wrestler, and on that occasion he meets Rosalind and falls in love with her at first sight. He also leaves for the Forest of Arden with his servant Adam. There, he regularly visits Ganymede (actually Rosalind) in order to be cured of his love for her. He marries Rosalind at the end of the play.

Adams is the old servant who faithfully follows Orlando into exile. There is a tradition that says that Shakespeare himself played this part. He silently disappears from the play.

Touchstone is a clown whom Rosalind calls a "dull fool." The dictionary definition of a touchstone is a stone used to test the purity of gold and silver. As Harold Goddard rightly remarks, "Shakespeare lets Touchstone judge himself in judging others." In the encounters with the shepherd, Corin, we see Touchstone's snobbery and his rudeness in contrast with Corin's pride and modesty. In the short interlude with Audrey, whom Touchstone will ultimately marry, he uses puns from mythological and literary spheres that completely and naturally escape her. Touchstone makes a fool of William, Audrey's former suitor, and even threatens him with death. He is the only fool in Shakespeare who marries.

Sir Oliver Mar-text is a vicar from another village whom Touchstone calls to marry him and Audrey.

Corin is a shepherd in the Forest of Arden who shows extraordinary insight in his own character in the verbal fight with Touchstone, who tries to disgrace him: "Sir, I am a true labourer: I earn that I eat, get what I wear, owe no man hate, envy no man's happiness, glad of other men's good, content with my harm."

Silvius is a young shepherd in the Forest of Arden who is in love with Phebe, whom he eventually weds.

William is the youth who lays claim to Audrey.

Rosalind is the central and dominating figure of the play. She is the daughter of the exiled Duke and cheerfully in love with Orlando. Disguised as Ganymede, she undertakes to cure Orlando of his love for Rosalind. She asks him to come every day and woo Ganymede as if he (Ganymede) were Rosalind. Rosalind and Orlando get married in the final scene. She is full of vigor and wit, and she controls the action of the play. Rosalind is as important to *As You Like It* as Hamlet is to *his* play. Although in love, she is able to see how love can change with time.

Her most memorable line is when she matter-of-factly says: "That men have died from time to time, and worms have eaten them, but not for love."

Celia is the daughter of Duke Frederick and cousin and devoted friend of Rosalind. She follows Rosalind into the Forest of Arden in the disguise of a shepherdess. At the end of the play she marries Oliver, Orlando's older brother.

Phebe is a shepherdess who falls in love with Ganymede (Rosalind in disguise) but finally marries Silvius, the man who loves her.

Audrey is a simple-minded country girl who cannot comprehend Touchstone's verbal wits. She, however, marries Touchstone. ❀

Critical Views on
As You Like It

SAMUEL JOHNSON ON SHAKESPEARE'S FABLE

[Dr. Samuel Johnson (1709–1784), the outstanding British literary figure of eighteenth-century life and letters, was a poet, essayist, critic, journalist, lexicographer, and conversationalist. His *Dictionary of the English Language* (1755) was the first major English dictionary to use historical quotations. In 1765 he wrote a monograph, *Preface to His Edition of Shakespeare,* and in the same year he edited a landmark annotated edition of Shakespeare's works. In this short extract Johnson speaks about play's qualities.]

> ROSALIND: His hair is of the dissembling colour.
> CELIA: Something browner than Judas's. Marry, his kisses are Judas's own children.
> ROSALIND: I' faith, his hair is of a good colour.

There is much of nature in this petty perverseness of Rosalind; she finds faults in her lover in hope to be contradicted and when Celia in sportive malice too readily seconds her accusations, she contradicts herself rather than suffer her favourite to want a vindication. ⟨ . . . ⟩

Of this play the fable is wild and pleasing. I know not how the ladies will approve the facility with which both Rosalind and Celia give away their hearts. To Celia much may be forgiven for the heroism of her friendship. The character of Jaques is natural and well preserved. The comic dialogue is very sprightly with less mixture of low buffoonery than in some other plays; and the graver part is elegant and harmonious. By hastening to the end of his work Shakespeare suppressed the dialogue between the usurper and the hermit and lost an opportunity of exhibiting a moral lesson in which he might have found matter worthy of his highest powers.

—Samuel Johnson, *Samuel Johnson On Shakespeare* (London: Penguin, 1765): 179–180.

WILLIAM HAZLITT ON ROSALIND AND CELIA

[William Hazlitt (1778–1830) is a British writer best remembered for his essays, which are read for sheer enjoyment of his brilliant intellect and for permanent value for their humanity. Among his many works are *Lectures on the English Poets* (1818), *Lectures on the English Comic Writers* (1819), and *Liber Amoris,* in which he describes the suffering of his love affair that ended disastrously. In this extract taken from his *Characters of Shakespear's Plays* (1817), Hazlitt contrasts Rosalind's and Celia's characters.]

Rosalind's character is made up of sportive gaiety and natural tenderness: her tongue runs the faster to conceal the pressure at her heart. She talks herself out of breath, only to get deeper in love. The coquetry with which she plays with her lover in the double character which she has to support is managed with the nicest address. How full of voluble, laughing grace is all her conversation with Orlando—

> —"In heedless mazes running
> With wanton haste and giddy cunning."

How full of real fondness and pretended cruelty is her answer to him when he promises to love her "For ever and a day!"

> "Say a day without the ever: no, no, Orlando, men are April when they woo, December when they wed: maids are May when they are maids, but the sky changes when they are wives: I will be more jealous of thee than a Barbary cock-pigeon over his hen; more clamorous than a parrot against rain; more new-fangled than an ape; more giddy in my desires than a monkey; I will weep for nothing like Diana in the fountain, and I will do that when you are disposed to be merry; I will laugh like a hyen, and that when you are inclined to sleep.
> ORLANDO: But will my Rosalind do so?
> ROSALIND: By my life she will do as I do."

The silent and retired character of Celia is a necessary relief to the provoking loquacity of Rosalind, nor can any thing be better conceived or more beautifully described than the mutual affection between the two cousins:—

> —"We still have slept together,
> Rose at an instant, learn'd, play'd, eat together,
> And wheresoe'r we went, like Juno's swans,
> Still we went coupled and inseparable."

The unrequited love of Silvius for Phebe shews the perversity of this passion in the commonest scenes of life, and the rubs and stops which nature throws in its way, where fortune has placed none. Touchstone is not in love, but he will have a mistress as a subject for the exercise of his grotesque humour, and to shew his contempt for the passion, by his indifference about the person. He is a rare fellow. He is a mixture of the ancient cynic philosopher with the modern buffoon, and turns folly into wit, and wit into folly, just as the fit takes him. His courtship of Audrey not only throws a degree of ridicule on the state of wedlock itself, but he is equally an enemy of the prejudices of opinion in other respects. The lofty tone of enthusiasm, which the Duke and his companions in exile spread over the stillness and solitude of a country life, receives a pleasant shock from Touchstone's sceptical determination of the question.

> "CORIN: And how like you this shepherd's life, Mr. Touchstone?
>
> CLOWN: Truly, shepherd, in respect of itself, it is a good life; but in respect that it is a shepherd's life, it is naught. In respect that it is solitary, I like it very well; but in respect that it is private, it is a very vile life. Now in respect it is in the fields, it pleaseth me well; but in respect it is not in the court, it is tedious. As it is a spare life, look you, it fits my humour; but as there is no more plenty in it, it goes much against my stomach."

Zimmerman's celebrated work on Solitude discovers only *half* the sense of this passage.

There is hardly any of Shakespeare's plays that contains a greater number of passages that have been quoted in books of extracts, or a greater number of phrases that have become in a manner proverbial. If we were to give all the striking passages, we should give half the play.

—William Hazlitt, *Characters of Shakespear's Plays: Lectures on the English Poets* (London: Macmillan, 1817, 1925): 188–189.

SAMUEL TAYLOR COLERIDGE ON AN UN-SHAKESPEAREAN SPEECH

[Samuel Taylor Coleridge (1772–1834), aside from being one of the greatest British poets of the early nineteenth century, was also a penetrating critic. His most famous critical work is *Biographia Literaria* (1817). In 1819 he delivered a series of lectures on Shakespeare, which were published posthumously in *Literary Remains* (1836–1839). In this extract Coleridge finds Oliver's speech (I, i, 145–54) to be un-Shakespearean.]

> OLI: Farewell, good Charles. . . . Now will I stir this gamester: I hope I shall see an end of him; for my soul, yet I know not why, hates nothing more than he. Yet he's gentle; never schooled, and yet learned; full of noble device; of all sorts enchantingly beloved; and indeed so much in the heart of the world, and especially of my own people, who best know him, that I am altogether misprized; but it shall not be so long; this wrestler shall clear all: nothing remains but that I kindle the boy thither; which now I'll go about.

This has always *appeared* to me one of the most un-Shakespearean speeches in all (the genuine works of) Shakespeare. Yet I shall be nothing surprised, and greatly pleased, to find it hereafter a fresh beauty, as has so often happened with me with the supposed defects of the great.

It is too venturous to charge a speech in Shakespeare with want of truth to nature. And yet at first sight this speech of Oliver's *expresses* truths which it almost seems impossible that any mind should so distinctly and so livelily have voluntarily presented to itself in connection with feelings and intentions so malignant and so contrary to those which the qualities expressed would naturally have called forth. But I dare not say that this *unnaturalness* is not in the nature of an abused *wilfulness* when united with a strong intellect. In such characters there is sometimes a gloomy self-gratification in making the *absoluteness* of the will (*sit pro ratione voluntas!*) evident to themselves by setting the reason and conscience in full array against it.

—Samuel Taylor Coleridge, *Shakespearean Criticism,* ed. T. M. Raysor (London: J. M. Dent, 1930): 93–94.

George Bernard Shaw on Shakespeare's Inaccuracy

[George Bernard Shaw (1856–1950) was an Irish dramatist, literary critic, and winner of the Nobel Prize for Literature in

1925 (he refused the award). Among his most famous plays are *The Devil's Disciple* (1897), *Caesar and Cleopatra* (1901), *Man and Superman* (1905), *Pygmalion* (1913) (adapted into a popular musical and motion picture *My Fair Lady*), and *Saint Joan* (1923). This extract is taken from Shaw's writings on the plays of Shakespeare. Here Shaw analyzes Shakespeare's statement "all the world's a stage" and the character of Rosalind.]

It contains one passage that specially exasperates me. Jaques, who spends his time, like Hamlet, in vainly emulating the wisdom of Sancho Panza, comes in laughing in a superior manner because he has met a fool in the forest, who

> Says very wisely, It is ten o'clock.
> Thus we may see [quoth he] how the world wags.
> Tis but an hour ago since it was nine;
> And after one hour twill be eleven.
> And so, from hour to hour, we ripe and ripe;
> And then, from hour to hour, we rot and rot;
> And thereby hangs a tale.

Now, considering that this fool's platitude is precisely the "philosophy" of Hamlet, Macbeth ("Tomorrow and tomorrow and tomorrow," etc.), Prospero, and the rest of them, there is something unendurably aggravating in Shakespeare giving himself airs with Touchstone, as if he, the immortal, ever, even at his sublimest, had anything different or better to say himself. Later on he misses a great chance. Nothing is more significant than the statement that "all the world's a stage." The whole world *is* ruled by theatrical illusion. Between the Cæsars, the emperors, the Christian heroes, the Grand Old Men, the kings, prophets, saints, judges, and heroes of the newspapers and the popular imagination, and the actual Juliuses, Napoleons, Gordons, Gladstones, and so on, there is the same difference as between Hamlet and Sir Henry Irving. The case is not one of fanciful similitude but of identity. The great critics are those who penetrate and understand the illusion: the great men are those who, as dramatists planning the development of nations, or as actors carrying out a drama, are behind the scenes of the world instead of gaping and gushing in the auditorium after paying their taxes at the doors. And yet Shakespear, with the rarest opportunities of observing this, lets his pregnant metaphor slip, and, with his usual incapacity for pursuing any idea, wanders off into a grandmotherly Elizabethan edition of the advertisement of Cassell's Popular Educator. How anybody over the age of seven can take interest in a literary toy so silly in its conceit and common in its ideas as the Seven Ages of Man passes my understanding. Even the great metaphor itself is inaccurately expressed; for the world is a playhouse, not merely a stage; and Shakespear might have said so without making his blank verse scan any worse than Richard's exclamation, "All the world to nothing!" ⟨ . . . ⟩

The popularity of Rosalind is due to three main causes. First, she only speaks blank verse for a few minutes. Second, she only wears a skirt for a few minutes (and the dismal effect of the change at the end to the wedding dress ought to convert the stupidest champion of petticoats to rational dress). Third, she makes love to the man instead of waiting for the man to make love to her—a piece of natural history which has kept Shakespeare's heroines alive, whilst generations of properly governessed young ladies, taught to say "No" three times at least, have miserably perished.

—George Bernard Shaw, *Shaw on Shakespeare*, ed. Edwin Wilson (New York: E. P. Dutton, 1896, 1961): 26–27, 29.

Harold C. Goddard on the Emersonian in Shakespeare

[Harold C. Goddard (1878–1950) was for many years head of the English department at Swarthmore College. He was the author of *Studies in New England Transcendentalism* (1906) and the editor of an edition of Ralph Waldo Emerson's essays (1926). One of the most important books on Shakespeare is Goddard's *The Meaning of Shakespeare*, published after his death in 1951. In this extract Goddard applies an Emersonian sentence to sum up *As You Like It*, and discusses Touchstone's character.]

There is generally an Emersonian sentence that comes as close to summing up a Shakespearean play as anything so brief as a sentence can. "A mind might ponder its thought for ages and not gain so much self-knowledge as the passion of love shall teach it in a day." There, compressed, is the essence of *As You Like It,* and, positively or negatively, almost every scene in it is contrived to emphasize that truth. As *Love's Labours Lost,* to which Emerson's sentence is almost equally pertinent, has to do with the relation of love and learning, *As You Like It* has to do with the relation of love and wisdom. Rosalind is the author's instrument for making clear what that relation is. 〈. . . 〉

When I read the commentators on Touchstone, I rub my eyes. You would think to hear most of them that he is a genuinely wise and witty man and that Shakespeare so considered him. That Shakespeare knew he could pass him off for that in a theater may be agreed. What he is is another matter. A "dull fool" Rosalind calls him on one occasion. "O noble fool! a worthy fool!" says Jaques on another. It is easy to guess with which of the two Shakespeare came nearer to agreeing. The Elizabethan groundlings had to have their clown. At his best, Touchstone is merely one more and one of the most inveterate of the author's word-jugglers, and at his worst (as a wit) precisely what Rosalind called him. What he is at his worst as a man justifies still harsher characterization.

In her first speech after he enters the play in the first act, Rosalind describes him as "the cutter-off of Nature's wit," and his role abundantly justifies her judgment. "Thou speakest wiser than thou art ware of," she says to him on another occasion, and as if expressly to prove the truth of what she says, Touchstone obligingly replies, "Nay, I shall ne'er be ware of mine own wit till I break my shins against it." Which is plainly Shakespeare's conscious and Touchstone's unconscious way of stating that his wit is low. And his manners are even lower, as he shows when he first accosts Corin and Rosalind rebukes him for his rude tone.

> TOUCH.:Holla, you clown!
> ROS.: Peace, fool; he's not thy kinsman.
> COR.: Who calls?
> TOUCH.: Your betters, sir.
> COR.: Else are they very wretched.
> ROS.: Peace, I say. Good even to you, friend.

Nothing could show more succinctly Rosalind's "democracy" in contrast to Touchstone's snobbery. (No wonder the people thought highly of her, as they did of Hamlet.) The superiority in wisdom of this "clown" to the man who condescends to him comes out, as we might predict it would, a little later.

TOUCH.:	Wast ever in court, shepherd?
COR.:	No, truly.
TOUCH.:	Then thou art damned.
COR.:	Nay, I hope.
TOUCH.:	Truly, thou art damned, like an ill-roasted egg, all on one side.

It is an almost invariable rule in Shakespeare, as it is in life, that when one man damns another, even in jest, he unconsciously utters judgment on himself, and the rest of the scene, like Touchstone's whole role, is dedicated to showing that he himself is his own ill-roasted egg, all "wit" and word-play and nothing else.

—Harold C. Goddard, *The Meaning of Shakespeare*, vol. 1 (Chicago: Phoenix Books/The University of Chicago Press, 1951): pp. 282, 285–286.

C. L. Barber on Touchstone's Praise of Folly

[C. L. Barber is the author of *The Whole Journey: Shakespeare's Power of Development* (1986) and *Shakespeare's Festive Comedy* (1959), from which the following extract is taken. Here he deals with *As You Like It* as one of the last two festive plays (the other one being *Twelfth Night*). In this extract he also discusses Touchstone's lines on time and Jaques' speech on the seven ages of man (in a different way than Shaw).]

As You Like It is very similar in the way it moves to *A Midsummer Night's Dream* and *Love's Labours Lost*, despite the fact that its plot is taken over almost entirely from Lodge's *Rosalynde*. As I have suggested in the introductory chapter, the reality we feel about the experience of love in the play, reality which is not in the pleasant little prose romance, comes from presenting what was sentimental extremity as impulsive extravagance and so leaving judgment free to mock what the heart embraces. The Forest of Arden, like the Wood outside Athens, is a region defined by an attitude of liberty from ordinary limitations, a festive place where the folly of romance can have its day. The first half of *As You Like It*, beginning with tyrant brother and tyrant Duke and moving out into the forest, is chiefly concerned with establishing this sense of freedom; the traditional contrast of court and country is developed in a way that is shaped by the contrast between everyday and holiday, as that antithesis has become part of Shakespeare's art and sensibility. Once we are securely in the golden world where the good Duke and "a many merry men . . . fleet the time carelessly," the pastoral motif as such drops into the background; Rosalind finds Orlando's verses in the second scene of Act III, and the rest of the play deals with love. This second movement is like a musical theme with imitative variations, developing much more tightly the sort of construction which played off Costard's and Armado's amorous affairs against those of the nobles in Navarre, and which set Bottom's imagination in juxtaposition with other shaping fantasies. The love affairs of Silvius and Phebe, Touchstone and Audrey, Orlando and Rosalind succeed one another in the easy-going sequence of scenes, while the dramatist deftly plays eadc off against the others. ⟨ . . . ⟩

But the liberty we enjoy in Arden, though it includes relief from anxiety in brotherliness confirmed "at good men's feasts," is somehow easier than brotherliness usually is. The easiness comes from a witty redefinition of the human situation which makes conflict seem for the moment superfluous. Early in the play, when Celia and Rosalind are talking of ways of being merry by devising sports, Celia's proposal is "Let us sit and mock the good housewife Fortune from her wheel" (I.ii.34–35). The two go on with a "chase" of wit that goes "from Fortune's office to Nature's" (I.ii.43), whirling the two goddesses through many variations; distinctions between them were running in Shakespeare's mind. In Act II, the witty poetry which establishes the greenwood mood of freedom repeatedly mocks Fortune from her wheel by an act of mind which goes from Fortune to Nature:

> A fool, a fool! I met a fool i' th' forest, . . .
> Who laid him down and bask'd him in the sun
> And rail'd on Lady Fortune in good terms, . . .
> "Good morrow, fool," quoth I. "No, sir," quoth he,
> "Call me not fool till heaven hath sent me fortune."
> And then he drew a dial from his poke,
> And looking on it with lack-lustre eye,
> Says very wisely, 'It is ten o'clock.
> Thus we may see.' Quoth he, 'how the world wags.
> 'Tis but an hour ago since it was nine,
> And after one more hour 'twill be eleven;
> And so, from hour to hour, we ripe and ripe,
> And then, from hour to hour, we rot and rot;
> And thereby hangs a tale.'
>
> (II.vii.12–28)

Why does Jaques, in his stylish way, say that his lungs "began to crow like chanticleer" to hear the fool "thus moral on the time," when the moral concludes in "rot and rot"? Why do we, who are not "melancholy," feel such large and free delight? Because the fool "finds," with wonderfully bland wit, that nothing whatever happens under the aegis of Fortune. ("Fortune reigns in gifts of the world," said Rosalind at I.ii.44.) The almost tautological inevitability of nine, ten, eleven, says that all we do is ripe and ripe and rot and rot. And so there is no reason not to bask in the sun and "lose and neglect the creeping hours of time" (II.vii.112). As I observed in the introductory chapter, Touchstone's "deep contemplative" moral makes the same statement as the spring song towards the close of the play: "How that a life was but a flower." When they draw the moral, the lover and his lass are only thinking of the "spring time" as they take "the present time" when "love is crowned with the prime." (The refrain mocks them a little for their obliviousness, by its tinkling "the only pretty ring time." But Touchstone's festive gesture is *not* oblivious. ⟨ . . . ⟩

Jaques speech on the seven ages of man, which comes at the end of Act II, just before "Blow, Blow, thou winter wind," is another version of the liberating talk about time; it expands Touchstone's "And thereby hangs a tale." The simplification, "All the world's a stage," has such imaginative reach that we are as much astonished as amused, as with Touchstone's summary ripe and rot. But simplification it is, nevertheless; quotations (and recitations) often represent it as though it were dramatist Shakespeare's "philosophy," his last word, or one of them, about what life really comes to. To take it this way is sentimental, puts a part in place of the whole. For it only is *one* aspect of the truth that the roles we play in life are settled by the cycle of growth and decline. To face this part of the truth, to insist on it, brings the kind of relief that goes with accepting folly—indeed this speech is praise of folly, superbly generalized, praise of the folly of living in time (or is it festive abuse? the poise is such that relish and mockery are indistinguishable). Sentimental readings ignore the wit that keeps reducing social roles to caricatures and suggesting that meanings really are only physical relations beyond the control of mind or spirit.

—C. L. Barber, *Shakespeare's Festive Comedy* (Princeton: Princeton University Press, 1959): pp. 223–226.

[Harold Bloom is Sterling Professor of the Humanities at Yale University and Berg Professor of English at New York University. He is the author of more than twenty books, including *Shakespeare, the Invention of the Human* (1998), and is the editor of over 400 anthologies and works of literary criticism. This extract is taken from his Introduction to *William Shakespeare's As You Like It* in the Chelsea House series MODERN CRITICAL INTERPRETATIONS. Here Bloom studies the character of Rosalind as Shakespearean inauguration of representation of personality.]

As You Like It is Rosalind's play as *Hamlet* is Hamlet's. That so many critics have linked her to Hamlet's more benign aspects is the highest of compliments, as though they sensed that in wit, intellect, and vision of herself she truly is Hamlet's equal. Orlando is a pleasant young man, but audiences never quite can be persuaded that he merits Rosalind's love, and their resistance has its wisdom. Among Shakespearean representations of women, we can place Rosalind in the company only of the Portia of act 5 of *The Merchant of Venice,* while reserving the tragic Sublime for Cleopatra. All of us, men and women, like Rosalind best. She alone joins Hamlet and Falstaff as absolute in wit, and of the three she alone knows balance and proportion in living and is capable of achieving harmony.

That harmony extends even to her presence in *As You Like It,* since she is too strong for the play. Touchstone and Jaques are poor wits compared to her, and Touchstone truly is more rancid even than Jaques. ⟨ . . . ⟩

Rosalind's spirit cleanses us of false melancholies, rancid reductions, corrupting idealisms, and universalized resentments. An actress capable of the role of Rosalind will expose both Jaques and Touchstone as sensibilities inadequate to the play's vision. Jaques is an eloquent rhetorician, in Ben Jonson's scalding vein, but Arden is not Jonson's realm; while Touchstone must be the least likable of Shakespeare's clowns. I suspect that the dramatic point of both Jaques and Touchstone is how unoriginal they are in contrast to Rosalind's verve and splendor, or simply her extraordinary originality. She is the preamble to Hamlet's newness, to the Shakespearean inauguration of an unprecedented kind of representation of personality. ⟨ . . . ⟩

Perhaps Rosalind's finest remark, amid so much splendor, is her reply when Celia chides her for interrupting. There are many ways to interpret: "Do you not know I am a woman? When I think, I must speak. Sweet, say on." We can praise Rosalind for spontaneity, for sincerity, for wisdom, and those can be our interpretations; or we can be charmed by her slyness, which turns a male complaint against women into another sign of their superiority in expressionistic intensity. Rosalind is simply superior in everything whatsoever.

—Harold Bloom, Introduction to *William Shakespeare's As You Like It* (New York: Chelsea House, 1988): pp. 1–4.

Plot Summary of
Twelfth Night

Twelfth Night or What You Will was probably written in 1601–1602, a year after *Hamlet* but before the other great tragedies. With nine comedies behind him, Shakespeare was at the height of his comic powers. For his setting he created the fictional world of Illyria, a country where everyone (except for Feste) is a little insane. Shakespeare might have turned to an Italian comedy of disguise and mistaken identity, *Gl'Inannati,* for his plot, but, as critics agree, no single work can be regarded as a direct source for *Twelfth Night.*

Orsino's, Duke of Illyria's, words on love open **Act I** and announce the main theme: "If music be the food of love, play on,/Give me excess of it, that surfeiting,/The appetite may sicken, and so die./That strain again! It had a dying fall." From the very beginning we are immersed into the intense maddening kingdom of Illyria. Orsino is in love with the Lady Olivia, who denies not only his suit but has given a vow to refuse the company of men for the next seven years because of the death of her brother.

Scene two opens on the seacoast where Viola is cast upon the shore of Illyria. Her twin brother, Sebastian, apparently was drowned during a great storm at sea. The sea captain befriends Viola and they both come up with the plan to disguise her in men's clothes and send her to Orsino's court to be his page.

In scene three at Olivia's house, Sir Toby Belch, Olivia's uncle complains to Maria, Olivia's gentlewoman, about St. Andrew Aguecheek, a wealthy nobleman who is brought by Maria to court Lady Olivia. Sir Toby is supposed to help him advance his courtship, but he never stays sober long enough to do so.

Scene four brings us to the middle of the action: Viola, disguised as Cesario, has become a favorite page at Duke's court. Duke Orsino finds her (him) to be a possible effective messenger to send to Olivia. Viola (as Cesario) agrees to do her best to woo his lady, but she has already fallen in love with Orsino herself: "Yet a barful strife! Whoe'er I woo myself, would be his wife."

In scene five Maria warns Olivia's clown, Feste, that Olivia wants to dismiss him. Feste, however, gains Olivia's favor, despite the ill will of Malvolio, her steward. When the Duke's messenger Viola (as Cesario) is announced, Malvolio denies her entrance. But Viola (as Cesario) will not accept it, and finally Olivia lets her approach. Olivia, however, falls in love with Cesario (so well played by Viola); by the end of conversation she sends Malvolio to give the youth a ring and to ask him to visit her the next day. Act I ends with Olivia's famous words: "Fate, show thy force! Ourselves we do not owe. What is decreed must be and be this so!"

Act II, scene one brings us back to the seashore where Sebastian and Antonio come ashore. Sebastian assumes that his twin sister, Viola, has been drowned. Although Antonio has many enemies at Orsino's court, he is determined to follow Sebastian out of the great affection he feels for him.

In scene two the play joins Malvolio as he is about to return the ring that Viola (as Cesario) supposedly left with Olivia. Viola (as Cesario) shows concern that "his" outward appearance might have charmed Olivia. Viola (as Cesario) tells her that for a poor lady it would be better if she loved a dream. Aware of how complicated the relationship has become, Viola (as Cesario) calls upon Time: "O Time, thou must untangle this, not I;/It is too hard a knot for me t'untie."

Scene three finds Sir Toby and Sir Andrew together with Feste the Clown and Maria, staying up late at night and making so much noise singing and laughing that Malvolio storms into their room. He is unsuccessful at calming them down, so goes off to report them to Olivia. Maria, in order to get revenge, suggests they trick him with a love letter, which he will think has been written by Olivia.

At this point the play moves to Orsino's languishing for Olivia (scene four). In a highly Petrachan manner, Orsino expresses his melancholy feelings and asks for music to accompany them. It is more than obvious by now that he is more in love with his own love than with Olivia. Still he presses Viola (as Cesario) to renew his suit. In a dialogue with the Duke, in very ambivalent terms, Viola (as Cesario) confesses her love for him, but it doesn't seem that the Duke understands it.

Scene five shows Sir Toby, Sir Andrew, Maria, and Fabian (another member of Olivia's household) plotting the fall of Malvolio. By placing a forged letter (supposedly written by Olivia) in which Olivia professes her love for someone who would "be opposite with a kinsman, surly with servants." She asks him to wear yellow stockings cross-gartered and smile constantly in her presence. Malvolio is taken in, to the delight of the conspirators, who look forward to his next meeting with Olivia.

At the start of **Act III,** Viola (as Cesario) returns to Olivia, who now shows hints of her love for Orsino's messenger. Viola (as Cesario) safely keeps her distance, but Olivia bids him to come back again.

In Act III, scene two Sir Toby persuades Sir Andrew, who grew restive after seeing Olivia's affection for the youth, that Olivia showed favor in his sight only to exasperate him (to put fire in his heart). Sir Toby suggests that Sir Andrew write a challenge to Cesario, to which Sir Andrew agrees. In the meantime Malvolio, following the instructions of the letter, dresses in the prescribed yellow stockings and garter and goes to see Olivia with a foolish smile on his face. Sir Toby follows Maria to observe the meeting.

From Olivia's garden and house, scene three moves to the street where Antonio gives Sebastian his purse. Sebastian wants to tour the city to see its "things of fame." Antonio, reluctant to be seen in Orsino's dukedom, leaves to find lodging and food at an inn called the Elephant.

In scene four, the action returns to Olivia's garden. Olivia is waiting for Viola (as Cesario), whom she has sent for. She decides that seeing Malvolio, her solemn steward, might please her. When Malvolio appears "yellow-stockinged and cross-gartered" and answers her questions by quoting sentences from her supposed letter (which are incomprehensible to her), she thinks he has been hit by a midsummer madness. She orders Maria to have her people take special care of him. Malvolio, however, still blind to her true reaction, thinks she loves him dearly. Sir Toby, Fabian, and Maria plan to have him bound and confined to a dark room.

Sir Toby presses the fearful Sir Andrew and Viola (as Cesario) into a duel. But as they unwillingly draw their swords, Antonio enters, and thinking that Viola is her twin Sebastian, goes to rescue his friend. At this point the officers of the Duke enter; one of them recognizes Antonio as an old outlaw and they arrest him. Antonio asks Viola (as Cesario) for his purse, but, to his amazement, Cesario denies any acquaintance with him whatsoever. Antonio feels betrayed by his friend, and, in the heat of his emotions addresses Viola (as Cesario) as Sebastian. Viola is left with the thought that Sebastian might in fact be alive: "Prove true, imagination, O, prove true,/that I, dear brother, benow ta'en for you."

At the beginning of **Act IV,** Feste, who is sent to find Cesario, instead finds Sebastian, who doesn't comprehend his message. Sir Andrew, Sir Toby, and Fabian enter, and Sir Andrew instantly attacks Sebastian, who draws, in contrast with Cesario, his sword readily and even wounds the knight, along with Sir Toby. Olivia enters and orders everyone away from Sebastian, whom she also takes to be Cesario.

In scene two Feste the Clown, disguised as Sir Topas, joyfully torments Malvolio, who is still locked up in a dark chamber. Sir Toby, however, would like to be out of the game.

In scene three the play joins Olivia as she is about to offer herself to Sebastian, who is baffled by the situation he is in. But Olivia's beauty and her position persuade him to accept the offer to marry her. The priest comes and they marry.

In the final scene (**Act V,** scene one) images of violence dominate: Antonio, before the Duke, relates his adventures with Viola (disguised as Cesario), who he thinks is actually Sebastian; Olivia enters and claims that Viola, who she believes is Cesario, is *her* husband; Orsino is absolutely aghast and threatens to kill Viola; Sir Toby and Sir Andrew break into the scene covered with blood and believing Viola is Cesario, blame her for their wounds. When Sebastian makes an entrance, the company sees what the audience has known all along: that Viola and Sebastian, twin brother and sister, are both alive: "One face, one voice, one habit, and two persons/A natural perspective, that is, and is not."

Viola changes into her maiden clothes, and Orsino, now recalling and comprehending Viola's utterances of affection, abandons his love for Olivia and marries Viola. We are told that Sir Toby will marry the energetic Maria, rewarding her for her witty plot, but we do not see Maria again. The gaiety of the play's end is darkened by the intrusion of Malvolio, finally released from his imprisonment, who swears vengeance upon them all with the unforgettable words, "I'll be revenged on the whole pack of you." Feste's sobering song closes the play, bridging the gap between the remote realm of Illyria and our own world. ✿

List of Characters in
Twelfth Night

Duke Orsino, Duke of Illyria, is a melancholy character, more in love with his love than with Lady Olivia, whom he courts. He marries Viola at the end of the play. The Clown Feste rightly remarks that Duke's mind is "a very opal," very changeable; he is, in some way "out of joint with his time" (Ruth Nevo), expressing his love in Petrarchan terms.

Olivia is a rich countess, "of beauty truly blent," who is in mourning for her brother and refuses the advances and company of men, including the courtship of Duke Orsino. However, Viola (disguised as Cesario), captures her heart. Olivia eventually marries Sebastian, Viola's twin brother.

Viola is the twin sister of Sebastian. After being cast ashore during a storm, she is in Orsino's service, disguising herself as a man named Cesario. She falls in love at first sight with Orsino and finally marries him at the end of the play.

Sebastian is Viola's twin brother, whom she thought to be drowned at sea. Olivia takes him to be Cesario and asks him to get married, which he, although baffled, does.

Sir Toby Belch, Olivia's uncle, is harboured in her house, intoxicated throughout the play, along with the clown Feste and Sir Andrew Aguecheek. He pretends to advance Sir Andrew's courtship to Olivia in exchange for money.

Maria, Olivia's gentlewoman, successfully plots against Malvolio by humiliating him before Olivia, for no reason other than the position he holds. As a reward for her witty plan, Sir Toby marries her at the end of the play. There is a kind of cruelty in her, as there is generally in Shakespeare's practical jokers.

Sir Andrew Aguecheek is a wealthy but foolish knight, who, pressed by Sir Toby, duels with Viola (disguised as Cesario) and later wants to duel with Sebastian, whom he takes to be Cesario.

Malvolio, Olivia's steward, is the antitype of the revelers. He is dedicated to work and thinks everyone should follow his example. He is confined to a dark room after Maria sets a shrewd plot for him. Since he is made to think that the love letter he has received was written by Olivia, he aspires to be "Count Malvolio." Mutual hatred governs the actions of Maria and Malvolio. Although he is humiliated out of proportion, he keeps his dignity in the encounter with disguised Feste.

Feste is Olivia's fool who sees through Olivia's grief. He disguises himself as Sir Topas to deceive Malvolio but also helps him to be released from his imprisonment. Detached from other characters, he is in control of his emotional powers.

Antonio, a sea captain and friend of Sebastian, is an outlaw who returns to Illyria out of his affection for Sebastian. ❁

Critical Views on
Twelfth Night

SAMUEL JOHNSON ON ORSINO'S PERSPECTIVE

[Dr. Samuel Johnson (1709–1784), the outstanding British literary figure of eighteenth-century life and letters, was a poet, essayist, critic, journalist, lexicographer, and conversationalist. His *Dictionary of the English Language* (1755) was the first major English dictionary to use historical quotations. In 1765 he wrote a monograph, *Preface to His Edition of Shakespeare,* and in the same year he edited a landmark annotated edition of Shakespeare's works. In this short extract, Johnson analyzes Orsino's speech on a natural perspective and the play as a whole.]

> ORSINO: One face, one voice, one habit, and two persons!
> A natural perspective, that is and is not.
>
> (v. i. 213)

A 'perspective' seems to be taken for shows exhibited through a glass with such lights as make the pictures appear really protuberant. The Duke therefore says that nature has here exhibited such a show where shadows seem realities; where that which 'is not' appears like that which 'is'.

This play is in the graver part elegant and easy in some of the lighter scenes exquisitely humorous. Aguecheek is drawn with great propriety, but his character is in a great measure that of natural fatuity and is therefore not the proper prey of a satirist. The soliloquy of Malvolio [III.4.65] is truly comic; he is betrayed to ridicule merely by his pride. The marriage of Olivia and the succeeding perplexity, though well enough contrived to divert on the stage, wants credibility and fails to produce the proper instruction required in the drama as it exhibits no just picture of life.

—Samuel Johnson, *Samuel Johnson on Shakespeare* (London: Penguin, 1765, 1989): p. 185.

[William Hazlitt (1778–1830) is a British writer best remembered for his essays, which are read for sheer enjoyment of his brilliant intellect and for permanent value for their humanity. Among his many works are *Lectures on the English Poets* (1818), *Lectures on the English Comic Writers* (1819), and *Liber Amoris,* in which he describes the suffering of his love affair that ended disastrously. In this extract taken from his *Characters of Shakespear's Plays* (1817), Hazlitt speaks about a constant infusion of the romantic and enthusiastic in Shakespear's comedy.]

This is justly considered as one of the most delightful of Shakespear's comedies. It is full of sweetness and pleasantry. It is perhaps too good-natured for comedy. It has little satire, and no spleen. It aims at the ludicrous rather than the ridiculous. It makes us laugh at the follies of mankind, not despise them, and still less bear any ill-will towards them. Shakespear's comic genius resembles the bee rather in its power of extracting sweets from weeds or poisons, than in leaving a sting behind it. He gives the most amusing exaggeration of the prevailing foibles of his characters, but in a way that they themselves, instead of being offended at, would almost join in to humour; he rather contrives opportunities for them to shew themselves off in the happiest lights, than renders them contemptible in the perverse construction of the wit or malice of others. 〈 . . . 〉

Shakespear's comedy is of a pastoral and poetical cast. Folly is indigenous to the soil, and shoots out with native, happy, unchecked luxuriance. Absurdity has every encouragement afforded it; and nonsense has room to flourish in. Nothing is stunted by the churlish, icy hand of indifference or severity. The poet runs riot in a conceit, and idolises a quibble. His whole object is to turn the meanest or rudest objects to a pleasurable account. The relish which he has of a pun, or of the quaint humour of a low character, does not interfere with the delight with which he describes a beautiful image, or the most refined love. The clown's forced jests do not spoil the sweetness of the character of Viola; the same house is big enough to hold Malvolio, the Countess, Maria, Sir Toby, and Sir Andrew Ague-cheek. For instance, nothing can fall much lower than this last character in intellect or morals: yet how are his weaknesses nursed and dandled by Sir Toby into something "high fantastical," when on Sir Andrew's commendation of himself for dancing and fencing, Sir Toby answers—

"Wherefore are these things hid? Wherefore have these gifts a curtain before them? Are they like to take dust like mistress Moll's picture? Why dost thou not go to church in a galliard, and come home in a coranto? My very walk should be a jig! I would not so much as make water but in a cinque-pace. What dost thou mean? Is this a world to hide virtues in? I did think by the excellent constitution of thy leg, it was framed under the star of galliard!"—How Sir Toby, Sir Andrew, and the Clown afterwards *chirp over their cups,* how they "rouse the night-owl in a catch, able to draw three souls out of one weaver!" What can be better than Sir Toby's unanswerable answer to Malvolio, "Dost thou think, because thou art virtuous, there shall be no more cakes and ale?"—In a word, the best turn if given to every thing, instead of the worst. There is a constant infusion of the romantic and enthusiastic, in proportion as the characters are natural and sincere: whereas, in the more artificial style of comedy, every thing gives way to ridicule and indifference, there being nothing left but affectation on one side, and incredulity on the other.—Much as we like Shakespear's comedies, we cannot agree with Dr. Johnson that they are better than his tragedies; nor do we like them half so well. If his inclination to comedy sometimes led him to trifle with the seriousness of tragedy, the poetical and impassioned passages are the best parts of his comedies.

—William Hazlitt, *Characters of Shakespear's Plays* (London: Macmillan, 1817, 1925): pp. 157–160.

CHARLES LAMB ON THE CHARACTER OF MALVOLIO

[Charles Lamb (1775–1834), English essayist and critic, was among the greatest of English letter writers and a perceptive literary critic. He is best-known for his "Essays of Elia," and *Tales of Shakespeare,* a retelling of the plays for children, which he published with his sister Mary Lamb. In this extract Lamb argues that Malvolio's character should be played with an air of Spanish loftiness.]

Malvolio is not essentially ludicrous. He becomes comic but by accident. He is cold, austere, repelling; but dignified, consistent, and, for what appears, rather of an overstretched morality. Maria describes him as a sort of Puritan; and he might have worn his gold chain with honor in one of our old Roundhead families, in the service of a Lambert, or a Lady Fairfax. But his morality and his manners are misplaced in Illyria. He is opposed to the proper *levities* of the piece, and falls in the unequal contest. Still his pride, or his gravity, (call it which you will) is inherent, and native to the man, not mock or affected, which latter only are the fit objects to excite laughter. His quality is at the best unlovely, but neither buffoon nor contemptible. His bearing is lofty, a little above his station, but probably not much above his deserts. We see no reason why he should not have been brave, honorable, accomplished. His careless committal of the ring to the ground (which he was commissioned to restore to Cesario) bespeaks a generosity of birth and feeling. His dialect on all occasions is that of a gentleman and a man of education. We must not confound him with the eternal old, low steward of comedy. He is master of the household to a great Princess, a dignity probably conferred upon him for other respects than age or length of service. Olivia, at the first indication of his supposed madness, declares that she "would not have him miscarry for half of her dowry" (3.4.65–6). Does this look as if the character was meant to appear little or insignificant? Once, indeed, she accuses him to his face—of what?—of being "sick of self-love"—but with a gentleness and considerateness which could not have been, if she had not thought that this particular infirmity shaded some virtues. His rebuke to the knight, and his sottish revelers, is sensible and spirited; and when we take into consideration the unprotected condition of his mistress, and the strict regard with which her state of real or dissembled mourning would draw the eyes of the world upon her house affairs, Malvolio might feel the honor of the family in some sort in his keeping; as it appears not that Olivia had any more brothers, or kinsmen, to look to it— for Sir Toby had dropped all such nice respects at the buttery hatch. That Malvolio was meant to be represented as possessing estimable qualities, the expression of the Duke, in his anxiety to have him reconciled, almost infers. "Pursue him, and entreat him to a peace." Even in his abused state of chains and darkness, a sort of greatness seems never to desert him. He argues highly and well with the supposed Sir Topas, and philosophizes gallantly upon his straw. There must have been some shadow of worth about the man; he must have been something more than a mere vapor—a thing of straw, or Jack in office—before Fabian and Maria could have ventured sending him upon a courting errand to Olivia. There was some consonancy (as he would say) in the undertaking, or the jest would have been too bold even for that house of misrule.

Bensley, accordingly, threw over the part an air of Spanish loftiness. He looked, spake, and moved like an old Castilian. He was starch, spruce, opinionated, but his superstructure of pride seemed bottom upon a sense of worth. There was something in it beyond the coxcomb. It was big and swelling, but you could not be sure that it was hollow. You might wish to see it taken down, but you felt that it was upon an elevation. He was magnificent from the outset; but when the decent sobrieties of the character began to give way, and the poison of self-love, in his conceit of the Countess's affection, gradually to work, you would have thought that the hero of La Mancha in person stood before you. How he went smiling to himself! With what ineffable carelessness would he twirl his gold chain! What a dream it was! You were infected with the illusion and did not wish that it should be removed! You had no room for laughter! If an unseasonable reflection of morality obtruded itself, it was a deep sense of the pitiable infirmity of man's nature, that can lay him open to such frenzies—but in truth you rather admired than pitied the lunacy while it lasted—you felt that an hour of such mistake was worth an age with the eyes open. Who would not wish to live but a day in the conceit of such a lady's love as Olivia? Why, the Duke would have given his principality but for a quarter of a minute, sleeping or waking, to have been so deluded. The man seemed to tread upon air, to taste manna, to walk with his head in the clouds, to mate Hyperion. O! shake not the castles of his pride—endure yet for a season, bright moments of confidence—"stand still ye watches of the element," that Malvolio may be still in fancy fair Olivia's lord—but fate and retribution say no—I hear the mischievous titter of Maria—the witty taunts of Sir Toby—the still more insupportable triumph of the foolish knight—the counterfeit Sir Topas is unmasked—and "thus the whirligig of time," as the true clown hath it, "brings in his revenges." I confess that I never saw the catastrophe of this character, while Bensley played it, without a kind of tragic interest.

—Charles Lamb, "On the Character of Malvolio" in *William Shakespeare: Twelfth Night, or, What You Will*, ed. Herschel Baker (London: Signet/Penguin, 1965, 1998): pp. 136–138.

HAROLD C. GODDARD ON SHAKESPEARE'S FAREWELL TO COMEDY

[Harold C. Goddard (1878–1950) was for many years head of the English department at Swarthmore College. He was the author of *Studies in New England Transcendentalism* (1906) and the editor of an edition of Ralph Waldo Emerson's essays (1926). His most important book is *The Meaning of Shakespeare* (1951). In this extract, Goddard compares Chaucerian and Shakespearan method.]

Twelfth Night! So far from being a casual title, it is one of the most revealing ones Shakespeare ever used, however aware or unaware he may have been of all it implied. For Twelfth Night, January 6—though it is something else too—marks the end of the Christmas festivities. In half-a-dozen senses Shakespeare's *Twelfth Night* brings festivity to an end. To begin with, it is the third and last of the poet's own farewells to "wit" (*Much Ado* and *As You Like It* of course being the other two). In a wider sense it is his farewell to comedy. It is his transition from prince to king, his rejection of "Falstaff," not for the purpose of ascending the throne and conquering France, but of becoming "king" in the sense of mastering the domain of tragedy and tragicomedy. It marks an end too in more than a personal and professional way. It marks the end of Merry England, of the great day of the great Tudor houses where hospitality and entertainment were so long dispensed, one of the ends even (if I may use that expression) of feudalism itself whose long-drawn-out death never permits the historian to put a finger on any particular hour or event and say, Here it finally died. With its own reference to the pendulum swing of things, the whirligig of time that brings in his revenges, it seems like an intimation of the Puritan revolution with its rebuke to revelry—down even to the closing of the theaters. Merry England after the Armada certainly has its points of difference from the America of the twenties after World War I. (In the amount of genius produced that difference is abysmal.) But it has its points of likeness too. There was a descent and, if in a different sense, a Great Depression in store in both cases.

Did Shakespeare know what he was doing when he wrote and named this play? Did he appreciate its irony? Not entirely, of course. We have to wait for history to read its ironies into literature as it does into its own facts. But if Shakespeare's own development means anything, *Twelfth Night* is merely the culmination and consummation of something he had been saying almost from the beginning. If in *The Two Gentlemen of Verona* he gives us two revealing specimens of the species gentleman; if in *Romeo and Juliet* he shows us to what tragedy the code of the gentleman may lead; if in *The Merchant of Venice* he exposes the hollowness, and even cruelty, lurking under the silken surface of a leisured society; if in all these plays and in *Much Ado About Nothing* and *As You Like It* he tears the mask off wit and word-play, he does all these things at once in *Twelfth Night* (except that the tragedy that emerges fully in *Romeo and Juliet* is here only hinted at), but does them so genially that his very victims were probably loudest in their applause. We can imagine the Elizabethan gentlemen swarming to see *Twelfth Night* and paying for the privilege! It is almost as if the dead man were expected to pay an entrance fee to his own funeral and enjoy the proceedings. The poet just holds the mirror up to nature and gets a more devastating effect than the fiercest satire could achieve. It is the Chaucerian method. Indeed *Twelfth Night* makes one wonder whether justice has been done to the indebtedness of Shakespeare to the spirit of his great predecessor as distinguished from his indebtedness to him as source in the narrower sense (as in *Troilus and Cressida*). In *Twelfth Night* at any rate Shakespeare does something similar to what Chaucer does in *The Legend of Good Women:* so sweetens the medicine he is administering to his victims (in Chaucer's case the women) that they swallow it as if it were the most refreshing draught.

—Harold C. Goddard, *The Meaning of Shakespeare,* vol. 1 (Chicago: Phoenix Books/The University of Chicago Press, 1951): pp. 295–296.

C. L. Barber on Madness and Disguise

[C. L. Barber is the author of *The Whole Journey: Shakespeare's Power of Development* (1986) and *Shakespeare's Festive Comedy* (1959), from which the following extract is taken. Here Barber comments on the "madness" of the play and compares Viola's and Rosalind's (from *As You Like It*) disguises.]

Olivia's phrase in the last act, when she remembers Malvolio and his "madness," can summarize the way the play moves:

> A most extracting frenzy of mine own
> From my remembrance clearly banish'd his.
>   (V.i.288–289)

People are caught up by delusions or misapprehensions which take them out of themselves, bringing out what they would keep hidden or did not know was there. *Madness* is a key word. The outright gull Malvolio is already "a rare turkey-cock" from "contemplation" (II.v.35) before Maria goes to work on him with her forged letter. "I do not now fool myself, to let imagination jade me" (II.v.179), he exclaims when he has read it, having been put "in such a dream that, when the image of it leaves him, he must run mad" (II.v.210–211). He is too self-absorbed actually to run mad, but when he comes at Olivia, smiling and cross-gartered, she can make nothing else of it: "Why, this is very mid-summer madness" (III.iv.61). And so the merrymakers have the chance to put him in a dark room and do everything they can to face him out of his five wits.

What they bring about as a "pastime" (III.iv.151), to "gull him into a nayword, and make him a common recreation" (II.iii.145–146), happens unplanned to others by disguise and mistaken identity. Sir Toby, indeed, "speaks nothing but madman" (I.v.115) without any particular occasion. "My masters, are you mad?" (II.iii.93) Malvolio asks as he comes in to try to stop the midnight singing. Malvolio is sure that he speaks for the countess when he tells Toby that "though she harbors you as her kinsman, she's nothing allied to your disorders" (II.iii.103). But in fact this sober judgment shows that he is not "any more than a steward" (II.iii.122). For his lady, dignified though her bearing is, suddenly finds herself doing "I know not what" (I.v.327) under the spell of Viola in her page's disguise: "how now?/Even so quickly may one catch the plague?" (I.v.313–314) "Poor lady," exclaims Viola, "she were better love a dream!" (II.ii.27). In their first interview, she had told the countess, in urging the count's suit, that "what is yours to bestow is not yours to reserve" (I.v.200–201). By the end of their encounter, Olivia says the same thing in giving way to her passion: "Fate, show thy force! Ourselves we do not owe" (I.v.329). And soon her avowals of love come pouring out, overcoming the effort at control which shows she is a lady:

O, what a deal of scorn looks beautiful
In the contempt and anger of his lip!
A murd'rous guilt shows not itself more soon
Than love that would seem hid: love's night is noon.
Cesario, by the roses of the spring,
By maidhood, honour, truth, and everything,
I love thee so . . .

(III.i.157–163)

A little later, when she hears about Malvolio and his smile, she summarizes the parallel with "I am as mad as he, / If sad and merry madness equal be" (III.iv.15–16). ⟨ . . . ⟩

The most fundamental distinction the play brings home to us is the difference between men and women. To say this may seem to labor the obvious; for what love story does not emphasize this difference? But the disguising of a girl as a boy in *Twelfth Night* is exploited so as to renew in a special way our sense of the difference. Just as a saturnalian reversal of social roles need not threaten the social structure, but can serve instead to consolidate it, so a temporary, playful reversal of sexual roles can renew the meaning of the normal relation. One can add that with sexual as with other relations, it is when the normal is secure that playful aberration is benign. This basic security explains why there is so little that is queazy in all Shakespeare's handling of boy actors playing women, and playing women pretending to be men. This is particularly remarkable in *Twelfth Night*, for Olivia's infatuation with Cesario-Viola is another, more fully developed case of the sort of crush Phebe had on Rosalind. Viola is described as distinctly feminine in her disguise, more so than Rosalind:

. . . they shall yet belie thy happy years
That say thou art a man. Diana's lip
Is not more smooth and rubious; thy small pipe
Is as the maiden's organ, shrill and sound,
And all is semblative a woman's part.

(I.iv.30–304)

When on her embassy Viola asks to see Olivia's face and exclaims about it, she shows a woman's way of relishing another woman's beauty—and sensing another's vanity: "'Tis beauty truly blent. . . . " "I see you are what you are—you are too proud" (I.v.257, 269). Olivia's infatuation with feminine qualities in a youth takes her, doing "I know not what," from one stage of life out into another, from shutting out suitors in mourning for her brother's memory, to ardor for a man,

Sebastian, and the clear certainty that calls out to "husband" in the confusion of the last scene.

—C. L. Barber, *Shakespeare's Festive Comedy* (Princeton: Princeton University Press, 1959): pp. 242–244, 245.

ANN BARTON ON MEANING IN THE NAMES

[Ann Barton is a professor of English at Cambridge University, and fellow of Trinity College, Cambridge. She is the author of *Shakespeare and Idea of the Play* and *Ben Jonson, Dramatist*. In this extract, taken from her book *The Names of Comedy* (1990), Barton discusses the meaning of the names in *Twelfth Night*.]

Both *Twelfth Night* and *Coriolanus* are, in different ways, highly self-conscious about naming and names. In the latter, however, Shakespeare adhered to normal tragic practice in taking over the names he found in Plutarch, while in *Twelfth Night*, he sought out his own. The nomenclature of the comedy is characteristically hermogenean, with a larger-than-usual admixture (in the below-stairs world of Olivia's household) of the cratylic which may owe something to Shakespeare's awareness, at this stage in his career, of Jonson's rival kind of comedy. Certainly the incidence of pejorative speaking names for major characters—'Malvolio,' 'Aguecheek,' 'Belch'—is for Shakespeare relatively high. Even more reminiscent of the early Jonson is the fact that none of the three could be said to contradict his name, as Feeble does, for instance, in *2 Henry IV*, or the unexpectedly sprightly Constable Dull in *Love's Labour's Lost*. Significantly, all three of them are involved in that most Jonsonian of activities, a gulling plot. This plot, moreover, unlike the benevolent one which unites Beatrice and Benedick in *Much Ado About Nothing*, but very like that which unmasks Parolles (another character transfixed by a name he never defies) in *All's Well That Ends Well*, has as its aim only the comic humiliation and exposure of its victim.

The onomastic mainstream of *Twelfth Night* is, however, the one usually associated with Shakespeare. 'Olivia,' 'Viola,' 'Maria,' 'Fabien,'

'Orsino,' 'Sebastian,' 'Antonio'—even 'Feste,' attached to a surprisingly thoughtful fool—are at most suggestive, in no sense judging characters or holding them captive. Nor, at least in the case of 'Maria,' 'Sebastian,' and 'Antonio,' are they unique to this play. Like Menander, Terence, and Middleton—and unlike Jonson—Shakespeare continually repeated character's names. Although his comedies are dotted with inspired coinages ('Shylock,' 'Dogberry,' or 'Aguecheek'), names which could not possibly designate more than one character, for the most part he seeks out neutral praenomens regularly employed by other dramatists of the time, and reuses them across a range of plays. There are, for instance, four comic characters in Shakespeare named 'Sebastian,' four 'Balthazar,' two 'Ferdinand,' four 'Helen,' two 'Claudio,' two 'Angelo,' three 'Katherine,' and no fewer than seven 'Antonio.' The majority of these are figures of some importance, who also have (in most cases) no discernable surnames to distinguish them from each other. 'Angelo'—what? 'Antonio'—who? Only intermittently, as with the Ford and Page families of *The Merry Wives,* or the 'Minolas' in *The Taming of the Shrew,* does Shakespeare say.

—Ann Barton, The Names of Comedy (Toronto: University of Toronto Press, 1990): pp. 95–96.

Works by
William Shakespeare

Venus and Adonis. 1593.

The Rape of Lucrece. 1594.

Henry VI. 1594.

Titus Andronicus. 1594.

The Taming of the Shrew. 1594.

Romeo and Juliet. 1597.

Richard III. 1597.

Richard II. 1597.

Love's Labour's Lost. 1598.

Henry IV. 1598.

The Passionate Pilgrim. 1599.

A Midsummer Night's Dream. 1600.

The Merchant of Venice. 1600.

Much Ado About Nothing. 1600.

Henry V. 1600.

The Phoenix and the Turtle. 1601.

The Merry Wives of Winsor. 1602.

Hamlet. 1603.

King Lear. 1608.

Troilus and Cressida. 1609.

Sonnets. 1609.

Pericles. 1609.

Othello. 1622.

Mr. William Shakespeares Comedies, Histories & Tragedies. Ed. John Heminge and Henry Condell. 1623 (First Folio), 1632 (Second Folio), 1663 (Third Folio), 1685 (Fourth Folio).

Poems. 1640.

Works. Ed. Nicholas Rowe. 1709. 6 vols.

Works. Ed. Alexander Pope. 1723–25, 6 vols.

Works. Ed. Lewis Theobald. 1733. 7 vols.

Works. Ed. Thomas Hanmer. 1743–44. 6 vols.

Works. Ed. William Warburton. 1747. 8 vols.

Plays. Ed. Samuel Johnson. 1765. 8 vols.

Plays and Poems. Ed. Edmond Malone. 1790. 10 vols.

The Family Shakespeare. Ed. Thomas Bowdler. 1807. 4 vols.

Works. Ed. J. Payne Collier. 1842–44. 8 vols.

Works. Ed. H. N. Hudson. 1851–56. 11 vols.

Works. Ed. Alexander Dyce. 1857. 6 vols.

Works. Ed. Richard Grant White. 1857–66. 12 vols.

Works (Cambridge Edition). Ed. William George Clark, John Glover, and William Aldis Wright. 1863–66. 9 vols.

A New Variorum Edition of the Works of Shakespeare. Ed. H. H. Furness et al. 1871.

Works. Ed. W. J. Rolfe. 1871–96. 40 vols.

The Pitt Press Shakespeare. Ed. A. W. Verity. 1890–1905. 13 vols.

The Warwick Shakespeare. 1893–1938. 13 vols.

The Temple Shakespeare. Ed. Israel Gollancz. 1894–97. 40 vols.

The Arden Shakespeare. Ed W. J. Craig, R. H. Case et al. 1899–1924. 37 vols.

The Shakespeare Apocrypha. Ed. C. F. Tucker Brooke. 1908.

The Yale Shakespeare. Ed. Wilbur L. Cross, Tucker Brooke, and Willard Highley Durham. 1912–27. 40 vols.

The New Shakespeare (Cambridge Edition). Ed. Arthur Quiller-Couch and John Dover Wilson. 1921–62. 38 vols.

The New Temple Shakespeare. Ed. M. R. Ridley. 1934–36. 39 vols.

Works. Ed. George Lyman Kittredge. 1936.

The Penguin Shakespeare. Ed. G. B. Harrison. 1937–59. 36 vols.

The New Clarendon Shakespeare. Ed. R. E. C. Houghton. 1938–   .

The Arden Shakespeare. Ed. Una Ellis-Fermor et al. 1951–   .

The Complete Pelican Shakespeare. Ed. Alfred Harbage. 1969.

The Complete Signet Classic Shakespeare. Ed. Sylvan Barnet. 1972.

The Oxford Shakespeare. Ed. Stanley Wells. 1982–   .

The New Cambridge Shakespeare. Ed. Philip Brockbank. 1984–   .

Works about
Shakespeare's Comedies

Auden, W.H. *The Dyer's Hand.* New York: Vintage Books, 1968.

Barber, C.L. *Shakespeare's Festive Comedy.* Princeton: Princeton University Press, 1959.

Barton, Anne (Anne Righter). *Shakespeare and the Idea of a Play.* 1962. Reprint. Harmondsworth: Penguin, 1967.

———. *The Names of the Comedy.* Toronto: Toronto University Press, 1990.

Bloom, Harold, ed. *William Shakespeare's As You Like It.* New York: Chelsea House Publishers, 1988.

———., ed. *William Shakespeare's The Taming of the Shrew.* New York: Chelsea House Publishers, 1988.

———., ed. *William Shakespeare's Midsummer Night's Dream.* New York: Chelsea House Publishers, 1988.

———., ed. *Shylock.* New York: Chelsea House Publishers, 1988.

Bradbury, Malcolm, and David Palmer, eds. *Shakespearean Comedy.* London: Edward Arnold Publishers, 1972.

Bradbrook, M.C. *The Growth and Structure of Elizabethan Comedy.* London: Chatto & Windus, 1962.

Bradshaw, Graham. *Shakespeare's Scepticism.* New York: St. Martin's Press, 1987.

Burckhardt, Sigurd. *Shakespearean Meanings.* Princeton: Princeton University Press, 1968.

Calderwood, James L. "*A Midsummer Night's Dream:* The Illusion of Drama." *Modern Language Quarterly* 26 (1965): 507–15.

Coghill, Nevill. "The Basis of Shakespearean Comedy." *Essays and Studies by Members of the English Association* 36 (1950): 1–28.

Colie, Rosalie L. *Shakespeare's Living Art.* Princeton: Princeton University Press, 1974.

Danson, Lawrence. *The Harmonies of "The Merchant of Venice."* New Haven: Yale University Press, 1978.

Empson, William. *Essays on Shakespeare.* Cambridge: Cambridge University Press, 1986.

Evans, Bertrand. *Shakespeare's Comedies.* Oxford: Clarendon, 1960.

Felperin, Howard. *Shakespearean Romance.* Princeton, N.J.: Princeton University Press, 1972.

Fergusson, Francis. *Shakespeare: The Pattern in His Carpet.* New York: Delacorte, 1958.

Frye, Northrop. *Anatomy of Criticism.* Princeton, N.J.: Princeton University Press, 1957.

————. *A Natural Perspective: The Development of Shakespearean Comedy and Romance.* New York: Columbia University Press, 1955.

Goddard, Harold. *The Meaning of Shakespeare.* Chicago: University of Chicago Press, 1951.

Greenblat, Stephen. "Marlowe, Marx, and Anti-Semitism." *Critical Inquiry* 5 (1978): 291–308.

Hill, R. F. "*The Merchant of Venice* and the Pattern of Romantic Comedy." *Shakespeare Survey* 28 (1975): 75–88.

Hollander, John. "*Twelfth Night* and the Morality of Indulgence," *Sewanee Review* 67 (1959): 220–38.

Kermode, Frank. *English Pastoral Poetry From the Beginning to Marvell.* London: Harrap, 1952.

————. "The Mature Comedies." In *Stratford-upon-Avon Studies* 3: *The Early Shakespeare,* eds. John Russel Brown and Bernard Harris (1961): 211–27.

Kirschbaum, Leo. *Character and Characterization in Shakespeare.* Detroit: Wayne State University Press, 1962.

Knight, Wilson. *The Shakespearean Tempest.* 1962. Reprint. London: Methuen, 1971.

Kott, Jan. *Shakespeare Our Contemporary.* 1964. Reprint. New York: Norton, 1974.

———. *The Gender of Rosalind.* Evanston, IL: Northwestern University Press, 1992.

McFarland, Thomas. *Shakespeare's Pastoral Comedy.* Chapel Hill: University of North Carolina Press, 1972.

Moody, A. D. "Shakespeare: *The Merchant of Venice."* *Studies in English Literature* 21 (1964).

Muir, Kenneth. *Shakespeare's Comic Sequence.* Liverpool: Liverpool University Press, 1979.

Nevo, Ruth. *Comic Transformation in Shakespeare.* New York: Methuen, 1980.

Spurgeon, Caroline. *Shakespeare's Imagery.* Cambridge: Cambridge University Press, 1935.

Stoll, E. E. *Art and Artifice in Shakespeare.* New York: Barnes & Noble, 1951.

Tillyard, E. M. W. *Shakespeare's Early Comedies.* Atlantic Highlands, N.J.: Humanities, 1983.

Wheeler, Richard. *Shakespeare's Development and the Problem Comedies: Turn and Counter-Turn.* Los Angeles: University of California Press, 1981.

Index of
Themes and Ideas